Too Good to Be True

ALSO BY BENJAMIN ANASTAS

An Underachiever's Diary
The Faithful Narrative of a Pastor's Disappearance

Too Good to Be True

A Memoir

Benjamin Anastas

New Harvest
Houghton Mifflin Harcourt
BOSTON   NEW YORK
2012

This edition published by special arrangement with Amazon Publishing

For information about permission to reproduce selections from this book,
write to Permissions, Houghton Mifflin Harcourt Publishing Company,
215 Park Avenue South, New York, New York 10003.

www.hmhbooks.com

Library of Congress Cataloging-in-Publication Data
Anastas, Benjamin.
Too good to be true : a memoir / Benjamin Anastas.
p. cm.
ISBN 978-0-547-91399-5 (hardback)
1. Anastas, Benjamin. 2. Novelists, American — 20th century — Biography.
3. Fatherhood. I. Title.
PS3551.N257Z46 2012
813'.54 — dc23
[B]   2012018994

Book design by Brian Moore

Printed in the United States of America
DOC 10 9 8 7 6 5 4 3 2 1

Too Good to Be True is a work of memoir. It reflects the author's present
recollection of his experiences over a period of years. Certain names,
locations and identifying characteristics have been changed. Dialogue and
events have been re-created from memory, and, in some cases, have been
compressed to convey the substance of what was said or what occurred.

Epigraph by F. Scott Fitzgerald, from *The Crack-Up,* copyright © 1945
by New Directions Publishing Corp. Reprinted by permission
of New Directions Publishing Corp.

For the Sustainers
and their Boy King
I.Z.A.

Contents

Well, when I had reached this period of silence, I was forced into a measure that no one ever adopts voluntarily: I was impelled to think. God, was it difficult! The moving about of great secret trunks.

— F. Scott Fitzgerald, *The Crack-Up*

Too Good to Be True

At the Church Door

IT TOOK A LONG time for me to admit that I had failed. Even as I write this, I can feel the old machinery kicking in and sputtering, "Yeah, but you still have time—" or "Don't worry, things will turn around—" or that old dependable excuse trotted out by the teenager in all of us: "The world just won't understand me." But I've stopped listening to my own excuses. I have reached the point in life where I no longer accept false hopes, the palliative care of counterfeit wisdom. Part of this is courage; even more is necessity. When you have failed like I have—that is, when you've watched all of your best-laid plans, one by one, fly off on their own like crazed songbirds and peel off in long, lovely arcs into the nearest picture window—then you'll understand how I ended up, one raw autumn day not too long ago, standing outside a church in Brooklyn with my hands pressed against the doors so I could pray. In broad daylight, arms spread like I was being frisked from behind, head bowed and murmuring pleas for help to a divine power I wasn't even sure that I believed in. A stalled career would be enough to get you there; I had that. A failed marriage; I had one of those too—the story of its undoing was so high-drama that I should have been a sultry Argentine in

1

a terry cloth robe, pacing my penthouse and arguing with a pre-op transsexual starlet on my product-placed mobile. The will to go on; it's not that I had lost it — no, I have never lost *that*, and I hope I never do — but everything I had worked for was vanishing and my losses were mounting and I was in need. I was in need. It's that simple.

So I found myself at the doors of the church nearest to where I live with my hands pressed against the cold exterior, asking, *Lord, I need Your help, show me a way out of this*, while a bus groaned up the street behind me and the sky threatened to spit rain, or an early snow, and my hands turned white from the cold. Nothing. I heard nothing. Just the bus. Failure thrumming in my ears. So I asked again: *Please, Lord, I need Your help. I am lost. My life is broken. Nothing works. Can You hear me? Nothing I try is working*, and again I heard no reply, only the farting of hydraulics as the bus receded down the street. I didn't stay there much longer. It was too cold. I opened my eyes, lifted my hands from the door, and plunged my fists in the pockets of my coat to warm them up. I turned and walked away. That's where this testament begins: if you've failed all the way up to the heavens, like I did that day, after failing in every way possible here on earth, then truth is the only medicine that you will tolerate. Because the truth is what you need.

Let's start right here: I am forty-one years old, of sound enough mind, though its habits have grown soft and its defenses weak from too much time spent traveling on what they used to call — remember? — the information superhighway, whether on my laptop with its glowing piece of violated fruit on the lid, or the awful little slab I've made the mistake of entrusting with my phone calls and, more and more, my higher faculties. Plato's Slab. It is the last metaphor. I can't stop touching my phone for another hit of dopamine, another fall into its time-erasing abyss.

The other night, while my phone lay coldly beside my pillow, I dreamed about it. I did. The Slab is always sending and receiving . . . I've had to stash its body deep in a utility drawer just so I could get this far; when my service contract is finally up, I'm going to drop my iPhone into an empty coffee can, fill it with wet concrete mix, let this coffin dry, then carry it to the nearest Genius Bar and see what they can do with it. For too long I have been peering into screens for messages and clues while my life — my life! — went virtual on me.

I don't have any time for more distractions. GPS, while it can help me find the nearest supermarket with a Coinstar machine, cannot guide me on the path to another life, cannot show me how to shrug off all the failures and repay all the debts that have brought me here. I will have to do it myself using older technology I find more reliable, simpler tools. I have something I want. I have *someone* I want. Actually, there's more to it: a child's bedroom that is empty on too many nights, an engagement ring I've been visiting in the boutique where it's for sale and asking the shopgirls in plaid flannel to take out for me. I have a notebook in my lap, the kind you steal from the office or buy in bulk from Staples, with a red left-hand margin, sea-blue lines, and cardboard backing. As soon as this notebook is filled, I will get another from the closet. There are plenty. I have all the pens in the house I could possibly use. Over the pages that will follow, and the time they will record, I can declare my regimen of losses over and start again; I can settle into a new life that is already here and waiting; I can make my peace, even if it's sad and a little bitter, with an undoing so complete it's hard not to step back and admire the symmetry of it. Someone else might call it "the return of the repressed." Or diagnose me with a case of "unconscious repetition." But I see other hands at work: The evidence of an artist. The fingerprints of a master who works in mirror images. How else can you explain waking up in a life that has come to resemble its earliest beginnings? That's what life wants: symmetry.

Or I can just give up. Go on screen-staring. Hit *refresh* over and over. I can stop this notebook right where I am, file it in a box with all the others I have abandoned, and go on losing.

Let's start with a little inventory. At the top, my unpaid bills.

Going Broke

I AM BROKE. Or to put it more decorously, like a writer with more leisure time and a better credit score would: midway through life's journey, I find myself lost in a deep wood and cannot pay my way back onto the straight path thanks to the burden of my debts and a steep drop in my yearly income. I've been broke before. It comes with the benefits package when you're a writer: we wait months for advances, years for royalties, and develop, over time, the incredible ability to divine the arrival of a letter carrier with a check based on tiny collisions between air molecules. But this kind of broke is new country. I am *Pilgrim* Broke. New World, Old Growth Forest as Far as the Eyes Can See Broke. I have 90 cents in the bank, $3 in singles in my wallet, and a small pile of change on the dresser beside my girlfriend's copy of Thomas Merton's *The Seven Storey Mountain*, which I've been reading before bed to calm my anxieties. Eliza is reading Stephen King's *The Stand*, a break from her usual fare of Leo Tolstoy and Henry James. Her financial life is on the upswing, so she can afford the diversion of a little horror. I'm too busy living a horror story of my own. My nerves couldn't take it.

"Oh God," she said with a little snort the other night, lying beside me in the lamplight. I turned away from Merton and saw her huddled over her book, an old hardback with browning pages. She was wearing the nightgown that's become my favorite in the year we've been together: a shirtdress in white Indian cotton, with embroidery and three buttons open at the neck. Her profile, especially in that light, looked like it belonged in a portrait by John Singer Sargent — she was my very own Madame X in a rent-stabilized three-bedroom in our favorite part of Brooklyn, which she found, by way of miracle, on Craigslist. We are still moving boxes in and out of storage, arranging furniture, hanging pictures, and settling in. My being broke has limited our choices and slowed the pace of making our new home complete. She had to cover my half of the rent this month. This has not been good for our relationship.

"He has that *thing* he always does," Eliza said, her nose still in *The Stand*. "It's like he can't help himself." She was starting to get wound up and shifted in the bed. Soon she would be gesturing emphatically. It was one of the first things that I liked about her: the gestures. Eliza cares freely, without regard for proportion, and she is not afraid to express it. "Just when you start to lose yourself in the story," she said, "he throws in something really juvenile."

"Like?"

Eliza lifted her knees higher and started hunting through for a passage. She was consumed, like she always is when she has a book in her hands. Watching her read is one of my favorite things. She goes somewhere far away. While I waited for her to find what she was looking for, I couldn't help wondering how much longer we would be poring over actual books — already, the brick of printed paper lying open at her knees, the cloth binding with its nicks and little stains, are in the process of being replaced by circuit boards and plastic, by books without pages a reader can ever touch or turn down at the corners, beamed from a gigantic server, through the air, to bedrooms very much like ours. I don't know whether these changes will help keep writing alive and well into the digitized future, or if my problems are an early warning that my profession is about to go extinct. In my bedroom, anyway, we still read books. The kind they make from trees.

Soon enough, Eliza found the passage she was looking for and read it aloud: "'God is great,' Mother Abagail said, 'God is good. Thank You for the sunshine. For the coffee. For the fine BM I had last night, You was right, those dates turned the trick . . .'"

I winced. "That's pretty bad."

"I know!" she said, waving the book at me in outrage. "It's awful!"

"When did he write that — 1978?"

"It's boy humor," she said. "You know what it makes me think of? A twelve-year-old boy with pimples and a hollow chest. Snickering at me."

"That was me when I liked Stephen King," I told her. "Definitely."

She tossed the book away and burrowed in next to me. "You're all grown up now, baby."

"That's sweet," I said. I burrowed back. "Do you want to hear some Merton?"

She nodded and stretched, squealing at the top. "Oh, I'm sleepy. Read to me."

We are no longer falling in love, the two of us; we are in love and getting used to living together. The high is not quite so addling these days, but sometimes when I look at Eliza across the breakfast table, or even on the subway platform while we wait (and wait) for the G train, a drowsiness comes over me that feels altogether new. It is the comfort that comes from trust; it is the mercy of all second chances; it is the slow-release narcotic dispensed from deep within the human organism when you have chosen someone and she has chosen you. It is a gift, and I am trying to keep it.

I was reading a passage from Merton aloud to Eliza, the book so ragged with underlining and flagged pages that it looked like I'd dropped it in the bathtub, when the phone at my bedside started vibrating. *Werrrrt. Werrrrt. Werrrrt.* I ignored it.

"The sky was bright and cold," I read. "The river glittered like steel. There was a clean wind in the street. It was one of those fall days full of life and triumph, made for great beginnings —"

Werrrrt. Werrrrt. Werrrrt.

"Shouldn't you get that?" she asked.

"Maybe."

I reached over and checked the number on the screen. It was a creditor, one of my craftier ones. They were in Dallas, but lately when they called, the area codes showed up local: 917 and 646. I was supposed to think it was an emergency at that hour and pick up even if I didn't know the number. I had to admit, it was a much better strategy than calling from obscure, distant area codes like 859 (Lexington, Kentucky) and 734 (Livonia, Michigan). That's what the taxpayer-supported credit mills usually did.

"It's not important," I said, and flipped the phone facedown on the dresser.

"Funny time to call," she said, her voice no longer sleepy.

The phone jumped, once more, with a voice mail. *Werrrrt.* I'd listened to automated messages from creditors so many times that I had them memorized by company and number. The message from Dallas was one of my favorites: *Benjamin AN-uh-STACE [sic]*, a simulated female voice said, *we have an urgent business matter to discuss with you. If this is Benjamin AH-nuh-STACE [sic], please contact us as soon as possible at 1-866-820 . . . This is the kind of call you get, in the middle of the night, when you have many mistresses, and they are all named debt.

"They don't take no for an answer," I said with a sigh.

"Who?"

"Creditors."

"Why are they calling in the middle of the night?"

"That's what they do," I said. "They call until you can pay. They're trying to make sure we have a conversation just like this," I added. "In our own bedroom."

"You're not paying your minimums?" she asked.

"No," I admitted. "Not right now."

"When can you?" I could see the panic in her eyes, feel the heat of it rising on her skin. It didn't help that her shoulder had slipped out of her nightgown and there were her freckles; the nearness of her body made my heart race. It always did.

"I don't know," I said. I sighed again. "Maybe in a few months."

Eliza doesn't hide her feelings well. In fact, I'm not sure I've seen her try. It's one of the qualities about her that I most admire, and I've often wondered, watching her let her emotions fly, how a person gets to be that way. She chalks it up to a good therapist, and I have to begrudgingly admit that she might be onto something.

"Do you want me to finish?" I asked, still holding *The Seven Storey Mountain* open in my lap.

"Okay," she said before rolling over on her side.

I was about to start reading again when Eliza flipped back over and said, "You promised me that you were ready."

"I know," I said. "I did promise."

She was looking straight at me, her eyes red at the corners from keeping her contact lenses in for too long. "I need you to hold up your end. I need to know that you can do this."

"I'm trying my best," I said. "I really am. I'm trying everything I can think of to get more work."

"A lot of women," she reminded me, "would have given up the first time you couldn't pay for dinner."

"I know that," I told her. "I once lost a girlfriend over a twenty-dollar cab ride. I realize how important money is."

"I can't live like this," she said.

"Okay."

"I really can't live like this."

If you have ever faced your own recession and spent your nights tossing in a sweaty tangle because you can't pay your bills, if you have been spurned at the ATM one too many times and feel dread when you enter your PIN, or if you have seen pity in the eyes of a waitress as she returns your declined credit card in a padded sleeve, then what I am about to share will be all too familiar. Still, you're encouraged to avert your eyes as I consolidate my "terrible small debts" in one place. (Thank you, F. Scott Fitzgerald, for the perfect phrase. I am too broke to have debts of real heft, real consequence.) First up, the government. I am on a payment plan, about to default, with the IRS for back taxes, a lucky $13K total. Every year I pay less up front than what I'll end up owing, and come April 15, I add what I can't shell out to my running tab — with interest. It's not what anyone would call financial planning, but it's the closest I've come to it since the bottom of my life fell out. I owe the Empire State a little sweat and blood ($1,400), currently being pinched from my checking account in monthly installments of $175; then there is my student load debt with Sallie Mae (a small fortune, $20K), a number that has actually grown in the twenty years since I finished school thanks to being bought and sold among lenders more than once and the eighteen-month hiatus I took from making payments while I was living abroad in Italy and more concerned with hunting for porcini mushrooms and picking olives. That's also when I started running up debt on my four credit cards ($12,000 total), a modest figure within the realm of recession-era horror stories, but paying all of them on time every month — believe me — has become a real unicycle act. Oh, and I also owe my accountant for last year's taxes ($450) and a therapist for three sessions she claims I never showed up for ($525) that were supposed to have been dedicated, in part, to helping me learn how to have a healthier relationship with money. I did meet with her in her office on the second floor of a Brooklyn brownstone that felt, to me, like a black site for the local food co-op. I should have known that I was in for trouble when, the first time she buzzed me into the vestibule, there was a clementine on the table and a sign on the wall instructing me to take off my shoes.

"Come up whenever you're ready!" a voice called from the top of the stairs.

After I had padded my way up in my socks and taken my place on a love seat in her office, the beaming therapist — her name was Sandi, and she must have been on quite a pharma cocktail — listened to me, nodding, in a patch of sunlight while I explained that I was broke and tired of it and I wanted to change my life. I wanted more time with my son, who had arrived in the world and been taken from me under conditions that were so surreal that I still had trouble getting my mind around them. (I will get to this soon; the story might fill an entire notebook, I'm afraid.) I wanted to finish writing a book instead of abandoning every one I started halfway through, a bad habit that I had been locked in since writing a novel that had been rejected by every publisher who read it except for a boutique house in Salzburg, cheating on my girlfriend at a book fair because I thought more love would make it feel better, getting married in a rush to try to magically dispel our problems with wedding vows, and losing my wife before our first anniversary to a revenge-affair-turned-real. I wanted to put my daytime-drama divorce behind me for good and fall in love again. When I was done talking, Sandi had fixed me with that look of gleeful empathy therapists get when they realize they've met an easy mark. She gushed. She complimented me. I remember a sound very close to purring. Before I knew it, I had agreed to her terms of treatment: she had a ten-session minimum, no sliding scale, and a strict twenty-four-hour cancellation policy. It sounded Draconian, but I thought I needed her. I must have had an Alexander Calder mobile of "issues" dangling over my head every time she beamed at me: MONEY/SELF-WORTH, DIVORCE WITH LINGERING GUILT, WRITER'S BLOCK, PART-TIME FATHERHOOD, FEAR OF STARTING OVER.

I hung in for as long as I could, showing up dutifully to listen to her lectures, delivered under a fruit bowl of curls, on overcoming stress reactions when I thought about my finances, using visualization techniques to open pathways to finding more income, and developing the habit of healthy "self-talk." I paid her in full every week, scrawling out a personal check on the love seat while she pretended not to watch, even if it just dug me deeper into overdraft. Finally, one morning that I remember for an odd smell in the air over Brooklyn, part baking bread and part natural gas, I walked to her brownstone, climbed the stoop at my appointed hour, and, instead of pressing her terrible buzzer, I bolted. I couldn't face telling her that she was out of my price range, and besides, I'd been distracted by the Band-Aid that had appeared on her forehead a few sessions back ("Just a routine biopsy," she explained) and I'd spent most of my therapeutic time since pondering what would happen if I reached up and pulled it off. Would the universe start pouring out? Or did Sandi's Band-

Aid conceal a minute recording device? These are a few of the thoughts that idled in my head while I waited on her love seat for the hour to expire. I am not proud of the way I ended my treatment, and I have every intention, once I can afford it, of making good on my balance. Still, it seemed strange to me then, and it still does now, that I went to her for help with my debt problem, and I only succeeded in owing more money.

I could go on with the scary numbers—and I could go on indefinitely—but I don't want to be a bore. Suffice it to say that I owe a king's ransom in medical bills thanks to the regular, ill-starred periods when I haven't been able to afford health insurance. One five-figure liability disappeared when St. Vincent's Hospital went under and my bill for emergency surgery was carted away into legal limbo. But the rest are alive and well and being pursued, as we speak, by lawyers from the finest firms in Suffolk County and a collections agent with a blunt charm named Ms. Lee. I owe back child support for 2010, a year I made so little money ($24,000—look at that number; now look at it again) that I am astonished to be free instead of locked away on the Deadbeat Dad wing at Riker's Island. I have borrowed money from my family, my friends, the ex-wife of a friend, Facebook friends, my own ex-wife, from Eliza, and from a corporate lawyer whom I met in a bar. I have current child support to pay, preschool tuition, presents to buy for the never-ending steeplechase of Brooklyn birthday parties, sneakers and snow boots and winter parkas to replace when there aren't any hand-me-downs. I have a roof to keep over my head, the refrigerator to fill, a want for coffee, the need for a working MetroCard so I can take my son to his preschool and ride the subway to freelance jobs and interviews. None of this makes me special. I realize that. Going broke is the same for everyone: the bills you met on time when you were making money start to go awry, one by one, until suddenly they snowball. The phone rings early, middle, and late with collections calls. The mailbox fills with notices that make you cringe on sight and change color the longer you go without answering them. You lose things, beginning with your credit and the freedom to choose, which comes with being bankrolled. Your clothes age badly. Your toothpaste tubes flatten, curl, and multiply on the sink. Your underwear droops, your white T-shirts turn gray, and your socks lose their rightful partners. "Can I go on?" you ask, wandering on the tether that comes from having empty pockets, and you do. The answer is always "yes," as long as you have something — or someone — to live for.

The other day I got a voice mail that I've saved on my Slab. I listen to it when another story pitch to a magazine editor goes unanswered, or when I've sent another cover letter and a copy of my CV to an encrypted e-mail address despite the near certainty that I will not be hearing back, or if I start to get dreamy as I go through another day of losses and slip into the spell that keeps me mired in the antigravity between the present and the past. It was a Friday. The night before, at some unknown hour, my four-year-old son — I called him Primo* when he was first born, and this private name of ours still fits — had woken up and come down the hall to our bedroom in his striped pajamas, tapping my arm and whispering "Daddy?" until I opened my eyes. I checked his PJs to see if he was wet (he wasn't, thankfully) and lifted him up onto the bed. He threw himself over me and nuzzled in for comfort. While I lay there beneath him like a pinned wrestler,

---

* The names in his world all belong to pop stars and demigods: Judd and Asta and Psyche and Cleo, Waylon and Soren and Slim. Instead of dropping acid or having serial affairs, like parents in the 1970s, my generation packages its yearnings in one-of-a-kind baby names.

wondering, in the dark, how he had managed to grow so long in so little time, I could feel that he was feverish. Nothing serious, my internal sensors indicated, but he was hot. He protested as I carried him to his room and tucked him back into bed; I took his temperature (99.8°F), delivered a dose of strawberry Tylenol, then kissed him good night on his clammy forehead. By that time, his eyelids were already falling shut and he was drifting off to the archipelago, populated by penguins and crisscrossed by monster trucks and double-decker buses, where four-year-olds spend their dreams.

In the morning, we kept him home from school. Eliza volunteered to stay with him so I could work, and together they hatched a plan to bake chocolate chip cookies, maybe do some watercolors while they were in the oven. It was new for me. I am used to being a single father. That means I have delivered the Tylenol, baked the cookies, and assisted with the watercolors on my own, often on a pauper's budget. I would never claim that being broke is beneficial, but it has freed me up to spend the one resource I do have on him, and on him alone: time. I have logged the hours in playgrounds and on subway rides, and we are closer because of it.

"You go to work, Daddy," Primo said, motoring past the kitchen, where I was dragging out my departure. "We're staying home today without you!"

The voice mail arrived at 12:36 P.M. I didn't get it until an hour later when I pulled my Slab of Darkness out of its quarantine and checked for calls, but the delay didn't matter. It wasn't urgent. Eliza and Primo were calling from home, where they were just sitting down, she reported, to a lunch of chicken soup with stars. The last batch of cookies was in the oven. They had turned out a little on the cakey side, but they still were a big hit. I could hear

Primo's spoon scraping his trucks-and-lorries bowl with every bite of soup.

"We're having a great day here," Eliza told me. "It's been so much fun."

"Hi, Daddy," Primo said breathily into the phone. "We're having stars."

It felt then — and it feels now — like a phone call from a future that has almost arrived, that I can glimpse and even stay in for a while, but there is no guarantee it's going to happen. Eliza is thirty-eight. We want to have children together while we still can. She loves me and she is wonderful with Primo, but she is practical, like most women I've known, and she doesn't have much time to wait.

"I thought," she tells me, "that you were ready for this. I thought you were more together."

What she means is, "I thought that someone who had published two well-regarded novels and wrote for glossy, influential magazines and taught at an Ivy League college and had a child to support would have at least a couple of twenties in his billfold instead of a pocketful of sweaty dimes and nickels." I don't blame Eliza for making that assumption, or for being worried about what kind of provider I will be for her and a baby — by any honest measure, I have been lousy at it. Well-intentioned, maybe, always giving of the money that I do have, when my cards are capitalized, but lately I've been forced to scrounge for hot dog money.

So here I am with this notebook, trying to keep my promises to the ones I love and find my way back from something close to ruin. I thought I was doing the right thing. I thought I was following a well-worn path. Most of us open our eyes at some point in our lives and find ourselves in a place we never would have chosen if we'd been paying more attention along the way—a region of unlikeness all the more disorienting because we have found it on our own, without anyone else to blame, propelled ourselves right into the maw of it by the force of our own desires. I step into my mine every time I check my bank balance online for the latest overdraft fee I've been charged for my troubles, or when I am reminded that soon—in just a few months—it will be a nice round decade since I published my last novel that anyone has heard of.

I don't have time to disguise this story for the sake of art, or the stomach to dress it up in false pretenses that will be more flattering to me or anyone else who plays a part. I will begin where I am. I will retrace the steps of how I got here with what I hope will be a sympathetic eye, and I will tell the story, though it is long and winding, as quickly as I can manage it. I will hole up as often as I can steal the time in a child's bedroom painted robin's-egg blue—the shade is Icy Moon Drops—toy vehicles garaged in every nook and cranny, play equipment overflowing from the windowsills, children's books of every size and shape shelved in a riot, a play tent propped in a corner for sleeping in when the regular bed is too "boring," or simmers with too much heat in the middle of the night. Primo is not here. On the nights when he is with us and the room is full, I'll find another place to go with my notebook. For now, I am sitting on top of his bedcovers, and everything I need is within reach; Eliza is outside the door, making her nightly rounds and using her own math to figure out how much longer she will stay. I can hear footsteps as she changes rooms, the hiss of the kitchen tap, the bubbling of her voice while she calls her family to check in and tells them everything is fine. Soon I will hear a knock at the door and it will open a crack.

"Are you all right in there?" she'll ask.

"Just working," I'll say.

"Will you be much longer?"

"A little while."

Time. If I only had more time.

Time to visit the glass elevator.

The Real Life of an Author

I LOST MY WIFE in a glass elevator at the Hilton in Frankfurt, Germany. Never mind that I hadn't exchanged my wedding vows with Marina yet, or tried on the ring that she had engraved with the prophetically impersonal message YOU ARE LOVED. Never mind that Marina wasn't in the elevator with me or even in the same country when I pressed the button to my floor and felt the car start to rise into the upper reaches of the hotel atrium — that it wasn't her face looking up at me for a first and long-awaited kiss, her waist trembling in my hands, her handbag sliding off her arm and landing on my foot. It wasn't Marina who touched my face as if to make sure that I was real and said, "*Ti amo*, Ben. *Ti amo*," and who would spend the night with me in the half-light of a high-rise in the middle of the city, in an airless double room on hotel sheets that felt all wrong against the skin. What was I doing there? It's not as simple as a fling in a foreign country that I thought I could get away with, though it did cross my mind that I would never have to tell another soul about the elevator ride. I loved Francesca too. If I had been craftier about it, or if having an affair had come more naturally to me, then nothing would have had to change from that day forward, nothing would have flown apart the way it did. The message I had engraved on Marina's wedding ring? It came from Dante: INCIPIT VITA NOVA. "A new life begins." That was my hope for us. Did I ever get it wrong. Not the new life part; the *kind* of new life. There was the life that ended when I stepped into the elevator with Francesca and pressed the button for my floor, knowing that she would spend the night with me, and the new and less familiar life that took its place.

It started with a book. I'd spent the last three years sweating out a novel that never found its voice and filled me with dread up until the day I wrote the final page. I had dreamed it up in a flush of confidence that came from having the kind of career I had always wanted by the age of thirty: my first novel had been a modest hit and there were still foreign editions coming out and a film adaptation in the works at a Hollywood studio; my second book had fulfilled the promise of the first and brought me into the fold of the most storied literary publishing house in the city; I was starting to publish regular book reviews in the papers that mattered and I often got cornered at sweaty parties in identical Brooklyn floor-throughs to discuss the finer points of Philip Roth or the merits of McSweeney's. I had arrived. At least, it felt like I was arriving. I knew what it was like to be envied by other writers who thought I had it made and to have strangers look up from their novel on the subway — *my* novel — and stare for a little too long while they tried to place me.

Marina was part of it. I had read her before we ever met: she had published a review of a novel by a bad-boy British author in the *Nation* that had made my heart race with its unexpected disclosures and the fearless energy of its arguments. The book was a roman à clef about the messy breakup between a successful novelist and film writer in London and the editor who is all but his wife. The writer trades in the solid adult life he shares with her and their two young boys for the freedom of being with a girl who plays in a rock band. The reviews of the novel in England had been savage, but Marina was not swayed by the consensus. She called the author a genius of the biographical tease, and she praised his ability to turn the details of his real-life breakup into both a work of literary art and a defense of love at any price. What had started out as an airing of the writer's dirty laundry became a tribute to the mind and its appetites, the punk-rock rebellion of the heart. She had singled out one line from the book to be the centerpiece of her review and meditated on its wisdom: "life without love is a long boredom." It was a book review, and a good one, full of unexpected leaps and bold opinions, but to me it seemed more like a love letter — to writing and its power to transform the muck of circumstances into something pure and universal, to the demands of an artfully lived life, to an ex-lover or an unknown reader out there on the other side. It felt like it was a love letter meant for me. I gripped the *Nation* so tightly while I read her review in my apartment that my sweat left fingerprint-sized stains on the newsprint. I called Marina a few days later out of the blue at the arts and culture magazine in Soho where she was working, and when I stuttered through an introduction she stopped me and said, "I know who you are! Geezum. Are you calling to make me all nervous?" We arranged to meet at a party later that week thrown by another magazine, and when I walked in and saw her waiting in an empty row of chairs after the reading, I thought, *Please let that be Marina*. It was Marina. I didn't have to worry. I sat down in the folding chair next to her and we grinned at each other for a long time without saying a word. The sum of her smile and her hazel eyes and her hair pinned up like a siren's in a film by Matthew Barney was heady. There was a cocktail party going on behind us, filled with friends and smart young editors on the climb, swirling wine in plastic cups and staring right through the huddling writers who orbited them while pretending not to, but neither of us cared. We sat there grinning at each other instead.

"Hi," she said, extending her hand for me to shake.

She said her name.

I said mine.

That was it.

I hadn't finished my second novel yet, but I was close. I was riding the wave of good fortune in book publishing that only comes, I now know, when you have yet to lose a dime for anyone. Three days a week, sometimes more if I was short on my rent, I trekked from Williamsburg to a penthouse on the Upper East Side where I did editorial work and drafted letters — the kind you put in stamped envelopes and send in the mail — for Oona, an eccentric publisher and patron of the arts, who had employed a long succession of promising young writers to keep her company and help her with her projects. I can still remember the first letter I wrote for Oona on the day she auditioned me, in an office behind the kitchen that I shared with her disgruntled chef:

Dear Woody,

You have my warmest congratulations on your wedding to Soon-Yi. I hope the occasion was a joy for both of you.

She liked my letters, and she appreciated my comfort with the absurd. It was crucial for the job. Normally she fired her secretaries on their first tryout, or at the smallest error or invasion of her privacy, but the bold-faced names in her Rolodex didn't awe me as they did others, and I had no trouble keeping out of her business. I had passed my first test with Oona, and I was allowed to stay on.

The word "apartment" hardly captures the scale of her place:

it was a manor house perched atop a discreet brick building on a private, high-security block on the East River, with a paneled elevator that ferried you to the door, a sweeping staircase piled with art books and auction catalogs and gifts that awaited wrapping or needed to be returned, and terraces on all sides with panoramic views of the East River and Manhattan. The art on her walls belonged in a museum, and it always surprised me, when I stopped to look at my favorite pieces — there was the relief that Oona called, simply, "the Duchamp," and one of Ed Ruscha's *The End* paintings — that I could get as close as I wanted without attracting the attention of a guard in uniform. Madame Chiang Kai-shek was a downstairs neighbor, living comfortably, I used to imagine, in a drug-addled dream where her husband was still fighting the Communists in China and she was still referred to in the papers as the most powerful woman in the world. Gracie Mansion, the mayor of New York's official residence, was just a stone's throw across a wooded park, and beefy chauffeurs in old-fashioned hats often idled on the block in Jaguars and blacked-out Mercedes. When Oona wasn't tied up with phone calls or catching up on proofs for the magazine she edited from deep in her bedroom, the chef would buzz me from the kitchen phone and call me into the dining room to join her for lunch with a single syllable, sometimes less. We sat together, with the light pouring through the windows facing the river, eating brightly colored soup with exotic garnishes, delicate medallions of fish on beds of froth. If Oona couldn't make it out of her bedroom in time for lunch or if she had appointments out, I was lucky to get a single cold artichoke on a plate or a sandwich with a few Ruffles potato chips that I ate at my desk. I used to go out on the terrace when I was alone in the house with a Diet Coke I'd grabbed in the kitchen, and I would look out across the water at Astoria and the industrial buildings along the river, or I would turn south and look down the length of Roosevelt Island and its brick wall of apartment towers toward the ghostly metal span of the Queensboro Bridge. The bridge looked like a broken toy from there, a plaything left behind by a mythic race of child giants that had once ruled the island and its waterways. Standing at the railing on Oona's terrace and watching the bridge in the distance, I used to whisper out loud a line from *The Great Gatsby* that I had learned by heart:

> The city seen from the Queensboro Bridge is always the city seen for the first time, in its first wild promise of all the mystery and the beauty in the world.

I was prone to bouts of romantic longing, and the city only made them worse. At my previous job, working in the president's office at a university in the Village, I'd followed a ritual whenever I got discouraged by all the typing and the filing and how long it seemed to be taking me to get my *real* life off the ground: at lunchtime I went up to Union Square, bought a sandwich from a deli, and sat in the park to have lunch in the shadow of 19 Union Square West. The building was nothing special; it was an office tower of a certain vintage, what Henry James would have called a "skyscraper" when it had first been built, but now it looked dwarfed and crowded in by the newer city growing up around it. The stone exterior was drab and soot streaked, the exact color (if it is a color) of a wet newspaper. Somewhere in that building, though, high above the square — or so I imagined — in a book-lined suite of offices smelling of old pipe tobacco and secret stores of whiskey, Farrar, Straus and Giroux was busy making books. I knew a little about publishing, but not much. I had an agent whom I talked to on the phone about the short stories that she was submitting for me, so far without a lot of success, and I had spent two years in Iowa when I was much too young to be in graduate school sitting in workshops led by writers I'd admired on the page before I considered that they might be real people who used urinals and didn't know how to drive a manual, and I had watched visiting luminaries glide in and out of town on the drafts of their reputations — one famous poet I picked up at the airport even asked to borrow my copy of *Songs About Fucking* by Big Black. ("I think I need to hear this," he said as he shoved the cassette in my tape player.) But still, no matter how many writers I saw sweating through their shirts at the podium or droning on for so long that people started muttering in their seats and gasping, "Oh, *come on!*" I still had trouble picturing myself in their place. I haunted bookstores whenever I could, gravitating to the new fiction shelf to check out the freshly minted authors and running my fingers over the gently curving spines in neat rows, pulling out the first novels that looked promising and opening them up to the creamy white title page, pausing there before I turned to the copyright and Library of Congress catalog information and scanned them for any clues that might be encoded there, a password that would gain me entry at the gates.

I kept a list in my head of the publishing houses that I wanted to work with the most. Farrar, Straus and Giroux was at the top. It was not just a publisher in my eyes; it was more like the Promised Land. Their books had a shabby, almost European elegance to them, like they knew they belonged on the bookstore shelf — if not in the window, where I often saw them sunning on their backs — and they didn't have to work too hard to get your attention. The authors won awards and prix and fellowships and medals; they looked haunted in their photos on the jacket, deadly serious about "the craft," as if they started each day by reading Faulkner's Nobel Prize address about the human heart in conflict with itself and spent the rest of their time laboring to keep literature alive for the ages. *We don't publish books*, FSG's motto went, *we publish authors*. I liked the way that sounded. It had been passed along to me on a fire escape somewhere in Queens by a poet who had been inside the offices once to meet an assistant he had asked on a lunch date. "National Book Awards?" he'd said with a knowingness that filled me with awe. "They paper the fucking place. It's like a shrine in there. You *whisper*." I fell silent in the middle of the party and let it all sink in. *We don't publish books, we publish authors.* I thought I knew what it meant. Or did I? I clung to this koan with the fervor of an aspirant who is waiting to be chosen, writing late into the night and in the morning before I went to work in self-inflicted solitude in order to become what I wasn't yet: *an author.* I wondered — as I sat on the benches in Union Square, my lunch spread out in my lap on white deli paper, the park's jumpy squirrels foraging for leftovers at my feet, and homeless men wheeling past with mountains of empties lashed down to their shopping carts, what kind of mysterious rite I had to pass through or conversion I would have to undergo before I could get up from the bench and leave the park and cross through traffic to 19 Union Square West and sign in with the bored security guard at his desk, letting it slip without looking up from his black binder, "FSG. I'm an author." Would it be anything like the Latvian solstice festival I had been to once in high school with my best friend, Michael, when I had stood in a clearing in the woods in New Hampshire and watched seventeen-year-olds vault over a ten-foot bonfire with their skin glowing and cigarettes still dangling on their lower lips as they flipped untouched through rising sparks and landed on the other side? Or would it be simpler and more sudden, like the message I had listened to on a pay phone outside a ferry station in Maine telling me that I had won the fiction contest at a men's magazine and they were publishing my short story in their next issue? I had celebrated with a pint of Ben & Jerry's that I ate in the shadow of a Dumpster while I looked out at the lobster boats slicing in and out of Bass Harbor at high tide, then I had climbed in my family's outboard and sped back across the channel as fast as 35 horsepower could carry me to the island where we had our summerhouse, grinning into the salt spray while the boat pounded over swells and not caring that I was getting soaked through and shivering myself blue in the sun and the wind.

It happened on a train. Marina and I had caught an afternoon Metroliner from New York to Union Station in Washington, D.C., at the same time that the bidding for my second novel was coming to a close. I didn't have a cell phone yet. Not everyone did then. I was still a few years away from the first phantom vibrations inside my pockets, the Pavlovian twitch when someone in the restaurant has the same ring tone. Marina and I were still too new to have raised the topic of living together, but I had started to spend most nights of the week at her apartment on Degraw Street in Carroll Gardens — all it took was one of the ironic "intifada" parties that the hipster Israelis in my building used to throw a floor below me before she had declared my place in Williamsburg unlivable. "Wow," she said to me the next morning, once we'd finally woken up with a debauched feeling that we hadn't earned, "I forgot what it's like to sleep over in the cool kids' dorm."

The trip to D.C. was our first as a couple. I hadn't planned it to coincide with the final round of bidding on my novel, but I was aware, as the train lurched out of Penn Station and broke into the light, that the excitement of closing a book deal while we headed down the Eastern Seaboard on Amtrak could only help my cause. One problem: I would need to use her cell phone. I had listened to it chirrup for attention from the depths of her handbag, and I had watched her squint at the numbers on the little screen when an incoming call interrupted our night, and I had waited a few paces away on the sidewalk, trying not to feel jealous, while she threw herself into a conversation with someone else *right in front of me*, but that was the extent of my experience with her Sony handheld. "The Thing," I called it. As in, "The Thing just rang." Or, "Do you have to bring the Thing?" Or, if she couldn't find it anywhere and looked stricken: "Don't worry, the Thing would never leave you."

"I just heard it," I told her early in the trip, somewhere at the mouth of New Jersey. We were sitting in our own four-seat suite on Amtrak, side by side. Marina had her wedges off and her feet rested on the windowpane. I could see her gigantic Ukrainian toes, the cartoonlike proportions of her feet that kept her planted to the ground in the yoga studio. They were not a flaw, those feet; they were her passport back to Odessa, her history. But the call. It was definitely the Thing.

Marina reached into her bag and rooted for the phone. "Hold on," she said. "I know it's in here . . ."

"Um," I said. "Can you hurry?"

She knotted her brow in concern. Her arm was missing up to the elbow. "Oh, dear."

"*Please?*"

Marina found the phone in mid-ring, thumbed one of its buttons, and pressed it to my ear. Then she beamed at me. "This is when you talk," she said. "Unless it's for me."

It was my new agent, Leo. He had good news. There were two bidders left in the running, both editors we'd targeted and whom I knew I wanted to work with. One worked at an imprint at Doubleday that published fiction I admired and read on my own; the other bidder was a rising young editor at Farrar, Straus and Giroux.

"Give me a number," Leo said.

I gave him a number. It wasn't high — a year's salary at Oona's magazine (I had graduated from writing her personal letters and worked at an office downtown as an editor) plus enough to take a research trip to Europe with Marina.

"Let me call you back," he said.

The phone rang again outside of Philadelphia. I was holding it this time. I'd had a hard time concentrating when I tried to read, so I just stared at the Thing and waited.

"What button do I press?" I asked Marina.

"'Button'?" she asked. "Did you say 'button'?"

"What's wrong with 'button'?"

"It's just wrong," she told me.

The phone kept on ringing.

"I need to answer!"

"It's a phone," she said, "not a elevator." She pointed: "There."

I pressed the little green phone and put the Thing to my ear.

"Hello?" I said.

It was Leo again.

"We've got your number," he said. "From both." I could hear one of the other agents in his office talking on the phone behind Leo. He had a second career as a TV actor and his voice was shrill enough to carry through concrete block. The bids had improved from the last call, Leo told me over the other agent's monologue, and they differed in ways that he would explain.

"FSG met the number?" I said. I wanted to be sure that I'd heard Leo right.

I had. They did.

"Where are you?" Leo asked.

"Philadelphia," I told him.

"Think about it," he said. "Call me back in Baltimore."

"But I don't need to think," I said to Leo. "It's FSG."

The monologue behind him kept going on. "Do it anyway," he said.

I looked at Marina beside me on the train. She was so excited for me that she was trembling. I was an author. I had Marina. I had an advance coming that was big enough to last me a year, maybe twice that long if other sales worked out. It felt like I had everything I'd ever wanted. It felt like I had everything.

There are secrets in publishing that no one ever tells you when you're young. Most books die at their first printing. That's the biggest one. Some of the books that die are roughly handled on their way to an unmarked grave at Potter's Field. Others die alone in shipping boxes and no one ever notices. There are the books that arrive with every promise of making their way, garlanded with quotes or launched with an assault on the airwaves — still they die like all the others. I remember when I got my first premonition that my novel might turn out to be the rule and not the exception: that it would be published to a faint chorus of reviews, some good and others mixed, a book party at a Chelsea gallery that would merit a line or two in a weekly industry roundup, a few readings at bookstores and performance spaces around town and a few more in other cities to four rows of chairs in the Cookbooks section of a Barnes & Noble or over the whirring of a blender making frozen coffee drinks on the other side of Diet & Health.

A year had gone by since Marina and I took that Metroliner to D.C. I had already quit my job. I was writing "full time," which meant that I looked for paying assignments most of the day and spent the rest of it trying to write. My manuscript had gone through rounds of careful edits and there was no more work to be done. I could only wait. And hope. I was at a recording studio somewhere in Midtown, where my publisher had booked me for an hour. They needed me to read from the book—just a few pages—for a CD that would be included with the advance reading copies (ARCs) they sent to booksellers. I'd chosen a passage from the novel that I thought would be a knockout. Ethan, my editor, agreed. I had practiced until I had the passage close to memorized and every emphasis and dramatic intonation in the right place. In the studio, I sat ready at the microphone. The pages I would read from were stacked and squared in front of me. The engineer in the sound booth had given me my instructions. The recording light went on. He pointed from behind the soundproof glass. I started reading. I could hear the nerves in my voice at first, but soon the language took over and the hint of a nervous tremor melted away. At some point while I read, the momentum of the scene building and the words rolling out of my mouth, I looked up from the page to see the engineer's reaction. He was fighting off a yawn behind the glass. It was a monster. That much I could tell. He rubbed his eyes while he listened on his headset. He sipped from a large deli coffee. He froze in his seat with a stricken look, and then it came. He yawned. It was one silent yawn in a sound booth in Midtown, but it carried on for months. It was contagious. I wrote a book. The world yawned. That's just how it is.

I still had Marina, though. I was enthralled. I couldn't believe my luck. The dot-com bubble was deflating all around us, giving the city an eerie, end-of-empire feel: strolling in the convection heat of summertime in Manhattan after dinner or a movie, clutching each other like addicts about to nod out, we passed office furniture heaped on the curb, huddles of aimless start-up geeks in expensive high-top sneakers and untucked shirts, bars exhaling a roar so profound from open doors that they had to be hosting a fabled "pink-slip party."

"Look," I said. "A sliver of the moon . . ."

"The moon? Where?"

"Right there, over the Yahoo! motel sign."

"Yahoooooo," she sang at the moon on Houston Street.

Broadband. Everybody was talking about it: How it didn't come fast enough. How broadband was the future. I used to scoff, "Poor suckers," every time I overheard the word on the subway or in the sweaty crush of a party. Who needed broadband? I already had Marina. Our life was better than anything in broadband . . . Soon we'd hatched a plan to leave New York and escape the steeplechase so we could write our books instead of getting lost in the pounding of hoofbeats on the turf, the plays for better position in the pack. Marina had just sold a book proposal for enough money to last us about a year in Italy if we were frugal; I had wires trickling in from foreign sales, and I would keep on writing reviews while I worked on a draft of my next novel. We took the leap. We did it blindly. The only thing we'd settled on was where to live: Marina's mother had a stone house in a medieval *borgo* in the wildest part of Tuscany that she'd bought at a good time for the dollar. It was in a little market town on a river known for its artisans, and the house stood empty for most of the year. We could live there rent-free for as long as we wanted, provided we did some upkeep. In the summertime we would share the house with Marina's mother, or we would travel instead — Marina spoke a sonorous Florentine that was rare among foreigners and ferried us through the country on a trail of flattery and compliments. It didn't seem possible that we could just get on a plane and move to Italy, but that was our plan. I had seven pages of my new novel written. That was it. I had written the pages in a single burst one morning and read them aloud to Marina on her couch ("That's great!" she had pronounced, beaming at me), but so far I hadn't been able to take the story any further. I wasn't worried, though; we were going to live in a village in the mountains. In the spring, the roadsides and the pastures gone fallow were covered in yellow broom and bright red poppies, and the farmers flew around the mountain roads on three-wheeled carts that sounded like lawn mowers, looking wild at low speeds. There was a six-hour clock on the stone tower looming over the village that chimed on an indecipherable schedule. There would be time. I would find my way into the book when I needed to.

Our retreat didn't go the way we'd planned. Marina wrote a draft of her book. That part turned out well. In my head I kept an encyclopedia of enchantments that I added to almost every day: watching a mushroom picker emerge from the woods in knickers and a blousy shirt one weekend that first fall, carrying a basket of porcinis in one hand while he yakked into his mobile phone; the chalet at the top of the Passo della Consuma where we stopped for *schiacciata con l'uva* and fortifying coffee on the way home from trips to Florence; the smell of woodsmoke that would settle over the valley on cold mornings; the chestnut festival in a town called Montemignaio, where they felled the biggest tree they could find, sliced its trunk into rounds, and burned from the inside out in the middle of the square on cold, clear nights, and the band, playing old-fashioned dance music, had to duck to avoid the sparks; stumbling into the parking lot of a hotel off the A1 highway with Marina and my friend Frank at first light after staying up all night in the lobby to watch the Arizona Diamond-backs beat the New York Yankees in game seven of the World Series. Spending a week during the olive harvest climbing into the branches of gnarled old trees on noisy ladders to coax the olives off by hand and listen to them drop on tarps and parachute silk spread below that the American GIs had abandoned in the same fields after dropping from their planes and landing. I was enchanted. It was hard not to be enchanted by our time in Italy. Even if living in an unheatable stone house in the middle of nowhere with Marina while our money ran out drove us both a little mad. I came down with *geloni*, a painful swelling of the fingers brought on by the constant, low-grade cold of the Tuscan winters; Marina had full-scale breakdowns from the isolation and the mold that kept growing back on the walls no matter how many times we scrubbed them or painted them with expensive *anti-muffa* paint. The house smelled like the inside of a pair of winter boots — and so did we. "I want to go home!" Marina would sob on the couch while another pot of beans simmered on the stove. It always happened at night, when the heat and the bubbling pot steamed the windows up from the inside. Outside it was pitch-black. "I want a real hot shower! I want to get dressed up in nice clothes and *go to a party*! I want to see a movie that isn't dubbed and doesn't stop in the middle for a break . . . I want to make money! I'm tired of being broke! I want to go to an office and sit at a desk and get a paycheck again . . ."

My book was going nowhere. I couldn't admit it to Marina, though. I couldn't admit it to anyone; I had trouble admitting it to myself. I couldn't face it. Instead, I submitted myself to a daily exercise in misery. Every morning I would open up my laptop and read over the pages I'd been working on the day before, trying to find a thread that I could pick up and follow that day while my mind was fresh from sleep and sharp from the first hit of coffee, trying to summon the right word, and then another, and then another after that, to fill the silence; the cursor would sit there blinking its eye at me, and I would feel my heart go cold with dread.

There was a persimmon tree outside the window of the bedroom I was using as my study. It grew in the yard of a neighbor of ours who didn't care about picking the fruit. For eighteen months I stared out the window at that persimmon tree when work was going badly and the hours crawled. I tried everything

I could think of to change the way I felt about the novel, to make it come alive: I wrote in longhand first, in the smallest writing I could manage, then I typed the finished chapters into my laptop; I filled the margins of my notebook with stacks of tiny sentence fragments that only I could read and left the pages blank; I gave up on the notebook altogether and typed my chapters on the computer screen in different fonts, in blue or yellow or red type. It was madness. I realized that. Trying to write a book that felt like it didn't want to be written was driving me mad. But still I went to that room every day and shut the door. I sat down at my desk and opened up the file I'd been working on. I *made* myself write the book. I *made* myself go back in there day after day to fight the same disheartening battle. And I watched the persimmon tree: it was late to fill with leaves in spring and looked kind of scraggly even at its fullest. Sometimes a flock of blackbirds settled in its branches and trilled away, but usually it just sat there empty, looking half-alive. In the fall the branches would swell with hard yellow fruit. Then the leaves fell off. The persimmons hung on the tree ripening orange and red, some of them pecked by birds, until they froze on the branches and started to rot. One by one they fell to the ground and shrunk into the earth. It was fruit that no living thing wanted, not even the birds. Not that much. I kept on writing.

I kept on writing.

"Is that a spreadsheet?" I asked.

"Yes."

I was having dinner with my agent, Leo, in Frankfurt. We were both in town for the annual Buchmesse, or "Book Fair": Leo to make deals for the writers his agency represented and me to run a board meeting for the literary nonprofit I had started working for after the money had run out and Marina and I came home to Brooklyn. The restaurant was bright, plush, and overbooked with pale publishing executives in precision European eyewear. I had jet lag and I was feeling far from precision myself—the only thing that helped was popping one of the Klonopin I had smuggled in my Dopp kit. We had a connection who worked in politics and had talked her way into bottomless refills for her prescription. I had spent the day wandering a circuit in the vast complex of exhibition halls and business centers where the fair took place, trying to manage my panic attacks. I hadn't been sleeping since I'd finished my book and dropped a copy off at Leo's agency in Chelsea with one of the assistants—usually when I finished a big project I felt a surge of elation followed by relief, but this time I had started worrying the moment I stopped writing. With good reason, as it turned out.

"I didn't know you kept a spreadsheet," I said to Leo.

Leo was busy reading through it while I watched. He kept the spreadsheet under the edge of the starched tablecloth, almost in his lap, so I couldn't see it.

"Is it that bad?"

"It's not good," Leo said while he flipped the page. I caught a glimpse of the front from across the table: the columns were all filled with publishers' names, dates, what looked like comments, and rows of boxes marked with an X. "We went wide with you this time. I'm just reminding myself if we're still out anywhere . . ."

Leo had just been to Majorca, where he had called me from a swimming pool to deliver the latest round of rejections ("I'm like Swifty Lazar now," he had quipped in the droll way he delivered all his lines. "Everything poolside."), and before that he had called me with bad news from the airport in Paris, and before that Leo had been out of the office for a vacation in Miami. Leo's suntan was like lacquer: glowing and multilayered. I'd never seen a Windsor knot quite as smooth and bulbous as his. It made me blush every time I looked at it. Leo had grown his hair out into a sculpted flyaway since the last time I'd seen him, smartly tinged with silver.

"I'm not showing this to you," Leo said when he had finished. He slipped the spreadsheet back into his briefcase. "The less writers know about the business the better. My job is to protect you from the idiots."

"I'm fine with that," I told him.

"Good."

The year before, my first time at the book fair, with my novel stalled around page 280 and my hopes for it in remission, I had followed my map of the fairgrounds into the wrong exhibition hall for a meeting with some Danes and found a regulation boxing ring set up at one end of the cavernous space. There was no explanation for the ring being there on the map or anywhere else I could find. People from the book fair trickled by on their way to use the public bathrooms or venture deeper into the hangar's sprawling neighborhood to do their business, hurrying down aisles in their suits and sensible shoes. I was tempted to climb into the ring and walk around, but I was running late for my meeting and I didn't want to miff the Danes. *What the hell,* I thought, and I climbed into the ring anyway. It was an easy hoist up with the help of the corner post. I stepped through the ropes. I had never been inside a boxing ring before and I took it all in: the empty square, the turnbuckles, the drooping ropes. Instead of a fight-night crowd on the other side, there was a hangar filled with booths and display shelves, a ceiling so vast that noise vanished into it. Heavy black curtains sectioned off the hall into smaller neighborhoods. No one seemed to notice that I was in the ring. It felt good to stand there on my own, peaceful. It wasn't long before I climbed down through the ropes and went off to find the Danes.

Something kept drawing me back to the ring as the book fair dragged on: I would wander over when I didn't have a meeting, buy a drink or a snack at the food stand that was right behind it, and see if anything was happening. Klieg lights went up overhead. A temporary wall was rolled in behind the ring. They started screening the movie *The League of Extraordinary Gentlemen* behind another wall of curtains and I could hear the rumble of action scenes and dubbed German voices—after a while, I even thought I could pick out the Deutsche Sean Connery.

Nothing else changed at the boxing ring. Until the morning the mystery was solved. I was headed for the strongest coffee I could find in the fairgrounds when I noticed a steady flow of people streaming in the direction of the hangar. I followed. I kept hearing the word "Ali." Posters had gone up everywhere advertising a book about Muhammad Ali called GREATEST OF ALL TIME, with photos of the boxer in his prime. It was a book promotion. Muhammad Ali was making an appearance at the Frankfurt Book Fair to promote a book. They even had an acronym for the project: GOAT. It seemed unfortunate to me. Who was the goat? Anyone who bought the book? Ali? Or was I the goat for coming to the book fair and discovering just how insignificant I was as a writer, just one name on the spine among the untold thousands, in a hundred languages, only dimly recalled by a handful of people? By the time I made it to the hall a crowd was already thronging the boxing ring. More fairgoers kept filing in the entrances. A swarm of TV cameras waited in the ring for Ali and press photographers lined the ropes. "*Ali! Bumaye!*" a faction in the crowd started chanting. "*Ali! Bumaye!*" A giant banner hung behind the ring with the title GREATEST OF ALL TIME in huge letters and the klieg lights blazed down from above. "*Ali! Bumaye! Ali! Bumaye!*" The chanting in the crowd built until it thundered. It sounded like nature. I watched while they wheeled Ali in for the main event under a spotlight. The crowd parted. "*Ali! Bumaye! Ali! Bumaye!*" It was hard to see much of anything through the entourage of bodyguards and handlers. They were dressed like pallbearers. Somehow they lifted Ali up into the ring. It took his entire entourage. "*Ali! Bumaye!*" He looked embalmed: dazed and shiny. They propped Ali in front of the cameras for his photo op. "*Ali! Bumaye!*" I couldn't stop watching, even though I wanted to. Ali teetered on his feet. He was sweating under the klieg lights in a sky-blue shirt. He struggled to lift his hands and took a feeble, slow-motion swing for the cameras. "*Ali! Bumaye!*" I looked around the hangar and all I saw were publishing functionaries. Hundreds of them. From entry-level assistants at their first book fair to sales reps for the paper dealers to upper management in a better class of suit. "*Ali! Bumaye!*" Waving their fists in the air and shouting in unison to the corpse of a great heavyweight they'd trotted out for the cameras before they propped him back in his luxury-appointed wheelchair and rolled him away. "*Ali! Bumaye!*" I had seen enough. I couldn't bring myself to join the cheering. I slipped out while Ali was still in the ring and wandered through the fairgrounds in a daze until I found myself, some time later, in the *biergarten* outside, chewing *weisswurst* and gulping beer from a plastic stein at a picnic table. I felt like Marlow in *Heart of Darkness*, or maybe it was Kurtz. I had walked into a hangar at the Frankfurt Book Fair and witnessed an event of immense darkness at the heart of the publishing industry.

"I had much higher hopes for you," Leo said across the table. "It's a terrific novel. Really terrific. Rough in some places, but you've matured as a writer. The response isn't what I expected."

"I'm not sure what I expected," I admitted. "But it wasn't this."

"Farrar wants a revise," he said. Leo was lapsing into agent-speak. It was a breezy, telegraphic language, rich in euphemism and coded meanings, that he used when he had bad news to deliver. He employed agent-speak at other times too, but never with the same ear for its music. Translation: FSG finally read your new book, and they rejected it too.

"They're committed to you," he went on.

Translation: You're on your own.

"We can discuss."

Translation: We can discuss it, but not right now. I'm too busy selling rights for my other authors. You're lucky I'm even sitting here.

"That was quick," I said.

Leo stared. It took me a moment to figure out why, but he was waiting for an explanation.

"Being an author, I mean," I went on. "It didn't last very long. You know: *We don't publish books, we publish authors.*"

I watched the sympathy rise up in the dark water of Leo's eyes. It was one of the things I liked about Leo: he only pretended that he wasn't human, that he hadn't come with the same unwieldy toolbox of convictions, hopes, insecurities, and doubts that his writers did. I never understood the value of trying to be more like a shark just because you had to swim with them, but then again, I wasn't an agent.

"You wrote a great book," he said. "It needs work. They all do. When this is over and you're sitting in your endowed chair twenty years from now, you might think it's the best thing that ever happened to you."

Leo propped up his chin with one hand and plucked my empty wineglass off the table with the other. He raised it in the air and started waving it in the direction of a waitress. His suit jacket was velvet. Or maybe it was the Klonopin that made it shimmer in the lemon-yellow light.

"There's an offer from the Austrians," he said, still holding up my empty wineglass.

"Really?" I asked, taken by surprise. "Should I be excited?"

"It's modest," Leo told me.

"How modest?"

"Modest."

Translation: Too small for me to mention a number. It would depress me.

"I can live with that."

He lifted the wineglass a little higher. "I'm waiting for best offer. Then we'll discuss. Right now I need St. Pauli Girl to come over here and get you a drink."

"Okay."

"She just saw me," he said. "Now she's going to another table." Leo put down the glass and let out a knowing sigh. "Service is really slipping in this country. They all come from Moldova now, you know."

My routine at the book fair was comforting in a way. In the morning I would choose one of the two suits I kept hanging in my closet and get dressed in the steam left over from the shower while CNN International played on TV. I would ride down the glass elevator into the lobby of the Hilton and have breakfast in the dining room, behind a wall of planters, before heading out to the metro station to join the regular commuters on their way to work. I had a tie on. I was carrying a leather briefcase. I had left my shoes outside the door overnight to be polished by the hotel staff. I used the automated kiosks to buy my metro tickets and I bought the *International Herald Tribune* from the same newsstand in the station every day. When the train stopped at the fairgrounds, I folded my paper under my arm and picked up my briefcase and joined the stream of traffic heading up the escalator from the station to the artificial city—complete with towers, auditoriums, TV studios, juice bars, restaurants, cafés, and a chilly outdoor beer garden—where I wandered through my days. I met with contacts from European foundations at their booths and exchanged brochures and business cards in the soft echo of the hangars. I carried printed matter through the halls in search of foreign publishers and agencies that my nonprofit could partner with, more and more people I could convince to sit down and listen to my script. I wandered too, just for the sake of wandering through the fairgrounds and taking it all in: the German hall with its walls of books arranged by author and incredible two-story displays; the Arab hall and the other book fair ghettos—Africa, Eastern Europe—with their poorer ventilation and paperbacks that looked like they'd been airlifted from the radical bookstores I'd been dragged to in the 1970s by my father in his leather sandals; the Italian pavilion with its smell of fresh-ground Illy coffee, chaotic all-day chatter, and trays of prosecco and bowls of bar snacks that would appear at the publishers' booths for happy hour at 4:30 P.M.

I didn't plan on being unfaithful. It hadn't even crossed my mind. But then I met Francesca. The Babel of the convention halls where we spent our days made it all too easy. I'd lost a book. That's not an excuse: it's just a fact. A book had broken me to pieces.

"I think it's brave," I told Francesca.

She was staring. "I can't believe it."

"It's not a nose anymore," I said. "There are parts missing."

Francesca seemed upset. "I only saw her yesterday! I really can't believe it."

We were sitting in the lobby of the Frankfurter Hof on an em-pire sofa, tucked between piles of coats that had been abandoned for the after-party raging all around us, and watching a scout with a collapsed nose tug on the necktie of a Spanish editor as they huddled under a chandelier, both holding flutes of overpriced champagne.

"I'm worried about the rest of it," I told Francesca. "It looks like it could go."

"It's not a full collapse," she said. "I saw that once in Mexico City. They're all mad for *cocaina* there. It's quite depressing."

"I love how she doesn't even care."

I could feel Francesca's warmth beside me. Everyone at the party was yelling to be heard and there was a DJ in a function room deeper in the hotel. "*Poverina*. I think she's very pretty."

"Unless you like a woman with a nose," I said.

"What?" Francesca's champagne flute was still almost full. Mine was empty. I'd been filling it regularly since we'd met at the party and now I'd reached my limit. "I didn't get that. It's so loud."

I leaned in closer on the sofa, my face brushing into her curls. "I was saying something stupid about her nose again. I can't help myself. I'm not sure why we're still talking about her nose. I can think of a thousand things I'd rather be talking to you about than a scout with a collapsed nose."

I could see the corner of her mouth curling up into a smile. Now that I knew what it felt like to be alone with Francesca in the middle of a party, on the last night of the book fair, I didn't want it to be over yet. I wanted to stay with her for as long as I could.

"Do you mean it?"

"Yes," I said. "I mean it."

"Tell me something else then."

"I think we should leave," I said.

43

"Why?" she asked, turning to face me. "Is there another party?"

"I mean I think we should leave together," I yelled.

"Did you say live together?" she asked, looking confused.

"Leave together! Let's leave together!"

"Good," she said. "That makes more sense than live together."

We sat there on the sofa for a moment. The din in the hotel was only getting louder.

"*Allora,*" Francesca said with a little sigh, "should we go?"

I never understood what glass elevators were made for, aside from the thrill of lifting off from the ground floor and climbing higher into a view. But now I know better. They are engines for making secrets, vehicles for creating symmetry. Inside, you are granted permission. *Go ahead,* they say. *Do it. You'll see.* I met Francesca at a dinner a long and expensive cab ride away from the Hilton, thrown by a British publisher I only barely knew. It was a German tavern with low ceilings and a menu written on chalkboards. I arrived late. I hadn't known many people in the crowd and I am sure that my discomfort showed; when I said my first hello upon walking in, Francesca had turned away from her conversation and looked up with a warmth that startled me. "Here," she said, leaning on the table with her thin brown arms, "come sit with me." We spent the entire dinner talking in the way that strangers sometimes do. Everyone else at the dinner was busy making rounds, getting up to have a smoke outside, and then coming back to a different seat, losing track of their wineglasses, sharing dinner dishes and napkins, switching their places so often that it was a different dinner party every time I remembered to look up. But not us, in our little hollow at the restaurant. Once we started talking, it was like we'd joined a conversation partway in and we needed to rush through the preliminaries to catch up. No one bothered us. The rest of the table was busy talking in a fever of intensity too. Except for the host. He grew more and more sullen as the night wore on, staring at Francesca over his glass of Fernet Branca and gradually turning the same color as his bright pink tie. He had made the announcement, earlier in the night, that he would drink nothing but Fernet Branca until Francesca made an offer for the Italian rights to a new novel about the London Blitz.

"You're making him suffer," I told her while the host listened, nodding with drunken gloom, to an agent who was leaning close and yelling in his ear. "Look at that. He's a beaten man."

Francesca shrugged. "I won't feel guilty. I read the novel and I didn't like it very much. I told him."

"You did?"

"Six hundred pages about the Blitz?" she asked. I was looking at her fingers on her wineglass. They were a student's fingers. Slim and awkward-looking, with bitten nails and little nicks from being clumsy. They were the only part of her that was like that, and I could tell she was ashamed of them. "It's much too heavy. The whole book takes place underground. Lots of rats and things."

"I like a post-Blitz novel better," I said. "You know. Rationing. Unexploded bombs in the garden. Maybe a Schiaparelli dress."

"Muriel Spark!" She slipped her hands around my arm all of a sudden and pinned me with her eyes. "You love her too?"

"I do," I said more quietly than I'd meant to.

"You know I met her once in Rome?" Her hands pulled away. I wanted them back. "She's an amazing woman. Possibly a witch." Francesca smiled as if this made her even more dear. "She's really quite scary. We talked about a few contracts and a book cover that she didn't like. After we met I kept losing things and finding them in hidden places. Is it hidden places?"

"Hiding places," I said.

"That's right," she said, "hiding places. I saw wild animals everywhere I went. Foxes and eagles in the middle of Rome. They were like her spies. I'm sure she put a spell on me."

I think we should leave, I said.

Is there another party?

I mean I think we should leave together.

Should we go?

Francesca was from Rome. You could see it in her brow, in the architecture of her nose. She didn't seem any more at home at a trade show in Frankfurt than I was, but she had an important job with one of the biggest publishers in Italy and going to book fairs to buy and sell rights was part of what she did. She had a boyfriend. They were engaged. They had been together since they were teenagers, young *fidanzati*, and nothing about him ever changed—she called him "Il Giovane Holden" after the Italian title of *The Catcher in the Rye*. It was his favorite book, she told me later, and it had crippled him. One minute he wanted to be a politician and run for local office as a Reformed Communist, the next he dreamed of opening a vegetarian restaurant that would be owned by a cooperative; for the last year he had been teaching elementary school in a mountain village two hours away and living with a family that took in boarders. He was hopeless, she claimed, but he was always happy. He had a child's gift for happiness, she said, and he could find it in the hardest places.

The story I told myself was simple: That love operates without reason. That it was foolish to try to understand it, or to pretend that I could control how it arrives or the hour it escapes. I could love Marina and want to marry her—we were engaged—and I could love Francesca too, with a different fervor, in the time we had together. I didn't think ahead to what it would be like to come home again and walk through the door with the glass elevator still on my skin: whether I would sit Marina down and tell her everything in the spirit of honesty and ask for her forgiveness, or I would try instead to keep it from her and go on as we'd been before. To lie, in other words. To let her marry into a lie. I wasn't worried about consequences — at least not yet. That would come later. At the airport, actually, while I was waiting in line at the security gate. It hit me like a stomach virus. *I just cheated on Marina. I had been unfaithful.* And now I had to deal with whatever it would bring. I almost crumpled. It was misery — real misery. I have felt it arriving all over again in every airport that I have been in since.

I wasn't worried yet, though. The glass elevator made sure of that. It was a comfortable place to dream freely. I had already made my confession to Francesca when we stepped in. I had told her on that first night at the restaurant that I had a girlfriend I lived with and that we were engaged. It didn't matter. That's the secret of affairs: there is something in us that seeks company in our wrongdoing. There is a deeper thrill when it's shared. Francesca only mentioned my engagement once, in the taxi we took from the Frankfurter Hof to the Hilton. It was late. The last night of the fair. I'd fallen quiet as soon as we got settled in the cab — it wasn't guilt or worry or the start of second thoughts. It was something else. I was grateful. When the cab pulled away from the curb and Francesca's head fell on my shoulder and she laid her hand on my chest, filling my eyes with tears and my nose with the smell of jasmine, I fell into a dreaminess that would carry me all the way to the hotel. *There's too much love in the world,* I thought. *How can there be so much of it?*

"Don't tell her," Francesca said on my shoulder. I rustled in my dreams.

"You don't think I should," I said.

"No." She said it just like that: *No.* "It's cruel."

She was right. It was cruel. But I did it. One night in bed I let it all tumble out while Marina was lying there beside me. It all came out. The full confession. *Tell her,* I'd admonished myself every night for weeks. *Just tell her.* Until I did.

It was warm inside the taxi. Francesca's head was on my shoulder. Frankfurt was all shuttered stores and empty office towers and banks glowing from inside like night-lights. I was still safe inside my dreaming. Francesca wasn't finished, though.

"You should get married," she said. "Don't call it off."

"I should?"

"Of course!" She didn't sound sad. Not at all. That was the strange thing. She nuzzled deeper into my shoulder. "It would be a pity not to do it now. A real pity."

"I'll think about it," I said.

She laughed.

"Why are you laughing?" I asked.

Her breath was warm on my neck. "Because that sounded very stupid."

"Thank you."

The taxi pulled up at the hotel. We paid. Francesca followed me through the doors into the gleaming marble lobby. There was a single attendant at the desk and he didn't look up from his computer screen when we passed through. I pressed the button for the glass elevator and the doors slid open. It had been waiting for us.

We stepped in.

Coinstar

I'M PICKING UP PRIMO at his preschool later for a two-night stay with us, and that means one thing: it's time for a visit to the Coinstar machine. I need to stock up on his favorite yogurt, milk, cereal, eggs, apple juice, and a blue bag of Pirate's Booty. The pantry at home is pretty well supplied thanks to the big shopping trip we made the last time I got a check, but these are Primo's staples. They are part of his routine when he is with me, and I do everything I can to store them in. Including scouring the closets and the kitchen drawers for forgotten change, collecting what I can find in a Ziploc sandwich bag, and carrying my stash to Coinstar — or the Penny Arcade; both accept the tiniest offerings, however tarnished, and redeem them into legal tender — for food money. I have no shame when it comes to resorting to the people's ATM. Perhaps I should. Until recently I had much higher standards for turning in change, waiting, at least, until my proceeds broke the $20 mark, but I've been going through one of those periods of late when I can't afford to maintain even that small dignity. I take what I have, calculating in my head what I'll need to buy each of Primo's staples, pour my baggie into the collecting tray, and hope for the best. The lowest I have gone so far is $8.41. That bought Primo's yogurt and a giant carrot, with a little left over for coffee. (I knew it was going to be bad, so I didn't bring him with me.) The cashier gave a little smirk when she saw the measly figure on my slip, but I didn't let it bother me. Coinstar is my miracle slot machine, a movable green altar to prosperity (at a 9.8-cent sacrifice for every dollar), and I have never been unhappy with my winnings.

I realize that I'm long past the age and the station in life where it's acceptable to carry around baggies of loose change. Tipping the tray into Coinstar and hearing the telltale rattle as the counter spins is not providing. It's not even getting by. It's losing. If I polled a sample of the people whom I'm closest to, I wonder how many of them have had to redeem change for calories within the calendar year. And out of those who have resorted to Coinstar for a meal, how many would admit it? I know that my father, who has considered being broke a protest vote against the American Dream for most of his life, would never submit himself to Coinstar. He would rather die than sift his coins into the belly of a beast that ate 9.8 percent of what he'd dropped in, and in front of everyone in the supermarket too. Certainly my grandmother, a lifelong saver of coins, buttons, sugar packets, mini shampoo bottles, and anything else of value, would disapprove of cashing in my change for short-term gain when I could sock it away and let it accumulate in the bank at interest. Eventually, I could use that same money to open a five-year CD — and then I'd really be living the dream of every hardworking Greek immigrant. Nana, wherever you are, and I hope it's at the reception desk of a nice office nestled on a fair-weather cloud over the Aegean: I'm sorry to embarrass you by bringing this up. It's not your fault. I should have saved the five-dollar bills we got from you every Christmas in envelopes from the bank with an oval cut out to show off Lincoln's portrait, the ones you took down from the mantel with so much pride, instead of blowing my money as soon as I could on video games and Cheetos. By now, I could be feeding Primo with it. That would have made you happy, and it also would have saved me the task of trying to wash the bitter smell of change from my hands in a preschool bathroom just the other day while Annabel, one of Primo's classmates, slipped inside the stall behind me to pee.

"You're Primo's daddy," she said behind the stall door.

"That's right," I said. "And you're Annabel."

"Why are you in here?"

"I'm washing my hands."

"I can do that."

"I bet you can. Once I'm all clean and dry, I'm taking Primo home."

"I'm peeing!"

Early in my relationship with Eliza, while I was teaching at two universities for $9,000 total in salary, finishing up a ghost-writing job for a Christian oilman that had kept me afloat for the year, trying everything in my power not to beg or borrow another dollar from anyone I knew, and visiting Coinstar when I needed a quick fix, I found this post on Facebook by a journalist who specialized in celebrity profiles for a glossy magazine. I had friended her in the big initial flurry of activity after I'd signed up, when I was trying to reach a personal milestone—one hundred or two hundred friends, I don't remember which—and I am pretty sure that we've never met in person.

what do you do with your old change? (I'm talking a vase full . . .)
February 14 at 5:35 p.m.

It was Valentine's Day weekend. Eliza was staying in a rented carriage house on an alley behind the main drag in Hudson, New York, a town I have always loved for its dissolute charm. She had only a few months left before she had to deliver a draft of her first novel to its publisher, so she had packed her library in a duffel bag, put her cat in his carrier, and smuggled him aboard Amtrak to the Hudson Valley for a working holiday. Primo was with his mother and the Nominee that weekend (I will explain her boyfriend's nickname in a little bit; the wait, I hope, will be worth it), so I had left the city and driven up to join Eliza in Hudson. I had just enough money for a full tank of gas, a Valentine's Day dinner for the two of us, and coffee in the morning. I'd be cutting it close, though, and if the restaurant was too pricey, there was a risk that I wouldn't have enough gas to get me home to Brooklyn. I was a prisoner of my own scarcity, as per usual. It wasn't as bad as the time, late that previous fall, when I had found myself in Midtown with nothing left in my wallet, no money on my Metro-Card, and no way of getting home except to ask a stranger for a swipe at the turnstile for the F train, or make the long trip home on foot. (I walked from Fifty-third Street to Park Slope, across the Brooklyn Bridge, in something like two and a half hours. I had to take it slow. Blisters.)

So you'll understand, maybe, why I was immediately taken in by the thread on Facebook when I saw it, devoted to the question of what the celebrity journalist should do with her "old change." I could see the vase on her dresser, one of the thin glass globes, I imagined, that come free with flower arrangements. It was full to the rim. Perhaps a little of her change had spilled over the mouth, leaving a halo around the globe of scattered riches; the layering of copper and nickel inside the vase would be undulating, like a desert rock formation, or a painting. I was almost breathless at my laptop, upstairs in the bedroom of the carriage house while Eliza worked on her novel a floor below. This was urgent. I knew what the celebrity journalist had to do. But someone else — a smiling man with a goatee — had already stepped in.

 ████████████ Take it to one of those machines at the supermarket and it'll give you paper money for it. (I think they keep a small %.)
February 14 at 5:37pm

 ████████████ Sounds like a plan! But I've never seen one in NYC. Anybody around here know if such a thing exists in the Big A?
February 14 at 5:38pm

Never seen one in NYC? Anybody know if such a thing exists? My heart sank. It seemed impossible. It couldn't be true. But then I read the celebrity journalist's opening post about her change again and checked her other recent posts, most about the musicals and other classic films she was watching, and I had to admit it: she sounded sincere. Maybe she was blessed, or incredibly hardworking, or so resourceful that it hadn't ever come to turning in her pocket change for groceries. Maybe she glided through her days on the upper tiers of currency and only used quarters for parking meters, tipping baristas, gumball machines. Then there was the alternative: the celebrity journalist needed the change, and the breezy tone of her initial post had been calculated to make it seem as if she didn't. In either case, from the time of the celebrity journalist's first post on Facebook asking the hive for advice about what to do with her change, it had taken only two minutes for her to get her first reply from the smiling man with the goatee. Two minutes. And more poured in from there. Despite the arm's length approach to Coinstar ("one of those machines at the supermarket"), I did feel partially vindicated. At least I wasn't the only person reading the thread who had a highly developed relationship to my pocket change.

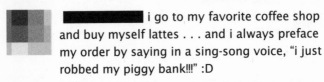

i go to my favorite coffee shop and buy myself lattes . . . and i always preface my order by saying in a sing-song voice, "i just robbed my piggy bank!!!" :D
February 14 at 5:39pm

I buy lottery tix w/ my change. ;-D
February 14 at 5:39pm

my parents bank has one of those change machines too, they r in nj, so maybe they have the same in ny, ill ask them
February 14 at 5:40pm

Ask your parents? I thought. *Really?* You don't need to ask your parents in New Jersey. I may not use emoticons or write in all lowercase or sing to my barista about how I broke my piggy bank, but I can tell you, the celebrity journalist, and the rest of her Facebook friends the precise location of every bank branch with a Penny Arcade below Fourteenth Street and a few more above that boundary too. They are trail markers for me, signposts for helping to navigate a city — and a life — that runs on lucre and all that it can purchase. My heart kept up its pitter-patter as I continued reading down the thread. I could hear Eliza downstairs, filling up another kettle for tea.

Some banks here in NYC do have them, and my once-every-few-years visits, pouring in a gazillion coins, more than anything else I do, make me feel like an excited child.

February 14 at 5:52pm

The post had been written by one of New York's media elite. He had edited magazines, founded Internet start-ups, written opinion columns on politics and culture, published novels that made it to the bestseller list. I didn't know the media insider personally, not well enough to call him a friend anywhere but on Facebook. He was as much of a mystery to me in life as the celebrity journalist. Marina had worked with him for a while on the relaunch of a design magazine, and we had been invited to the same dinner party once. This was back in flusher days. I was still working for the nonprofit and had visions, on my good days, of finishing the novel in a sudden flurry of inspiration and selling it for six figures. Marina was consulting for the magazine and waiting for her book to meet the world. It was a good memory, what I could recall from that dinner party: *bagna cauda* bubbled in a fondue pot on the coffee table, the wine flowed freely, we talked of restaurants and the upcoming presidential election and current writing projects and gentrification worries. The stuff of media professionals and opinion makers, people who weren't busy counting their own change. I have to admit, the media insider's post on Facebook bothered me. It spoiled my afternoon. I shut my laptop. I stood by the window and looked down on the little backyard behind the carriage house, with its flattened gardens, empty clothesline, and footprints in the snow. I am not often envious, no matter how low into the negative my bank account dips. Envy, of all the Cardinal Sins, comes about as naturally to me as anger and greed do, which is hardly at all. But I couldn't help thinking, while I stood at the window, of the media insider's gazillion coins jingling in the bank lobby and how nice it must have been to need reminding of the childlike excitement, the innocent pleasure, that comes from being rich.

Thanks to an unexpected bounty of change from a jar in Eliza's office, I decide to hit the Penny Arcade and to bring Primo with me. By all rights, visiting the Penny Arcade with a four-year-old should be a scene right out Mayberry. We'll waltz into the bank branch with our bag of coins, use the counting machine to tally up our savings, stand in line together with our slip, the excitement building, and stand in awe at the counter—Primo in my arms, straining to see—while the teller counts out our take in crisp virgin bills and freshly minted change. Mayberry had no banks, however, as squalid and rapacious as mine. There was a time, back when they were new in the market and were trying to make inroads, when coming into a branch was almost a pleasure and sitting down with one of their agents at a shared workspace felt like banking in a more egalitarian country. Like Sweden, if it annexed the population of Queens. I'd opened an account with them to escape an abusive relationship with Chase, which had been fleecing me for years with their service charges and fees. For a while I was happy. My checking account cost me virtually nothing. They cleared deposits the next day, no matter the size or how far the check had traveled. They gave away pens, lollipops, dog biscuits. And then there was Penny Arcade, admittedly a gimmick—I cringed every time the cartoon kid on the touch screen yelled, "Gee, you sure saved up a lot of coins!"—but it delivered an implicit message that appealed to me: We don't care how much or little you earn, where you come from, or how fraught with stress your financial history is. We'll take your money. You earned it. It has *value*, even if your last bank turned up its nose at your tarnished change and pushed it back at you through the window in its bulletproof sheathing.

My honeymoon lasted a while, with only minor slippages in fees, transaction charges, and customer service. The bank multiplied. Penny Arcade was a breakout hit. So were the bank's extended hours, which were duplicated by the competition. Then overnight, the bank changed its name. The color signature went from red and blue to green, just green—the color of the same money that it started bleeding from me with $35 overdraft fees. I hate them now. They are indifferent to me, even if, on the day that Primo and I visit the bank branch closest to his preschool with our sack of coins, they have shaken me down for more than $3,000 in service charges, penalties, and interest for the current calendar year. That's the price the broke pay for playing the zero line, and it's entirely legal. I have the added insult of having to explain to Primo, on our way inside from the street, what the glowing ad box in the window featuring the smiling, disembodied heads of Regis Philbin and Kelly Ripa means.

"What's she saying, Daddy?" Primo asks from my arms. I am trying to balance him, a tote bag with books for the subway and after-school snacks, his backpack, and our bag full of change, which is in danger of breaking.

"'Dogs are some of our favorite customers,'" I read aloud from the sign. "See," I say, pointing my elbow at the bottom of the ad, "that's a dog biscuit."

"Why are dogs some of their favorite customers?" he asks, gazing deeply into the ad, as if it holds a great secret. Maybe it does.

"It's a slogan," I tell him. "They give out free dog biscuits and put down water bowls in every branch."

"Why?"

"That's just what they do, I guess." He is slipping in my arms, so I bounce him up once to get a better grip around his bottom. The change clanks. "They treat dogs like people, and people like dogs."

"Daddy!" Primo squeals. He gives me one of those full-faced smiles that travel straight to my lizard brain. The gauze falls over my camera lens. When I look at him in close-up now, he is all soft and shimmery, like a four-year-old romantic lead in an old Hollywood star vehicle.

"All right," I backtrack. "Maybe they just like dogs."

"Why do they like dogs, Daddy?"

"Let's go in and do the change now," I suggest.

"I don't want to!"

"C'mon, we're going in."

The one Penny Arcade machine in working order at the bank that night has seen better days. It is deep inside the branch, near the corridor where tellers have a way of disappearing for long stretches in the middle of a transaction and the regular post for the police officer who stands there looking lost all the time, presumably as a deterrent against bank robberies. The crowd is sparse at that hour. The darkness in the windows lends a middle-of-nowhere feel to the branch. We could be in a mall on the outskirts of Albany, or on board a spaceship. The customer service desks are all cleared and vacant. There are only a few tellers left, busy doing tallies and ignoring the customers who come in. I put Primo up on the Penny Arcade machine, clearing away some of the day's debris from the counter first. It reminds me of the seating area of a bus station: hundreds of people must have emptied their vases and Ziploc bags and tea tins and pockets here. I see lint and thread and old subway tokens and bobby pins. I wonder if someone has actually been sleeping on the Penny Arcade; could someone just come in and lie down on top of the machine and sleep? It feels, to me, like a place where someone has been sleeping. Some banks here in NYC do have them, and my once-every-few-years visits, pouring in a gazillion coins, more than anything else I do, make me feel like an excited child.

Luckily, Primo doesn't seem to be aware of the human imprint. He just wants to pour the coins into the tray.

"I wanna do it!" he hollers.

"I'm just helping you a little," I say. "Here."

"I wanna do it all by myself! No, Daddy!" I let him keep the bag of coins in his lap and spill them out into the collection tray by the handful. That keeps him busy. I follow the steps by tapping on the touch screen, and we're in business. We shovel in our coins together, listening to them drop into the machine's gullet, and then I point out to him the display of numbers — a fake version of our tally — spinning on the screen.

"Wow," Primo says, eyes glued to the numbers. "Look at that!"

"I know," I say. "It's like a slot machine."

"Are we getting a lot of money, Daddy?"

"Well, I wouldn't say a lot."

"How come?" He sounds disappointed.

"That's all we have."

"How come we aren't getting a lot of money, Daddy? How come?"

"We have plenty for groceries," I say. "And you know what? We're getting *you* a bag of Pirate's Booty."

I pick him up off the coin machine and he tries to squirm away, keeping his head turned to watch the numbers spinning on the screen. It is the end of a school day; he is tired, probably hungry, and in one of his edgy, borderline cranky moods.

Primo doesn't often stump me with his questions. No matter what he asks, whether it's the constant volley of "whys?" that help him learn about the world, or any one of the odd technical questions that arrive out of nowhere ("What's fluoride, Daddy?"), I usually have some kind of answer for him, even if it's incomplete or turns out to be wrong when I think of it later and resort to Google. He stumped me the first time he ever memorized a joke (Primo: "How does a pig shovel gravel?" Daddy: "Let me see. I don't know. How does a pig shovel gravel?" Primo: "With a shovel!") and I am sure that many of my answers to his questions about NASCAR engines are useless. But at Penny Arcade, while the last of our borrowed coins rattle through the counter, I find that I have no answer when he asks me why we aren't getting a lot of money. I can't tell him how come we don't have a gazillion in change to cash in, other than the fact that we don't have it. I am confronted with the reality of being a broke father, and I am reminded of all that I am in danger of losing because of where I am. This makes me gloomy.

Gee, you sure saved up a lot of coins! It's the dickish little mascot, Penny, from the innards of the counting machine again, pretending that it's on my side while its employer screws me, keeps me coming back for more.

"I wanna go, Daddy," Primo whines.

"We need to get our slip and wait in line," I say.

The tears swell in his eyes. "But, Daddy! I wanna go!"

And so our outing to the Penny Arcade ended in tears (his), a bruised ego (mine), and a respectable $39.83 haul for groceries. Enough for what I needed that night, but not for what I want—not even close. Besides, I had paid too high a price for the trip in wounded pride. That's how it works at the Bank of Desperate Times: you walk in with your offering, pour it into the computing machine, and walk away with another debt against your soul's collateral, another figure to repay at interest. This time I owe my son.

Please, let him not remember.

Let that trip to the Penny Arcade be our last.

Unless it's for the joy of it. Not because I need to feed him, keep him in milk, yogurt, additive-free turkey bologna.

Let him know what it's like to have a father who can pay his bills.

Let him never have to ask, once he's old enough to know the difference:

Daddy, how come you're always broke?

Divorce Counseling

I'M A MONSTER.

When I stepped off the glass elevator, I had no idea that it would bring me here: to the windswept corridor of a high-rise in Manhattan, sixteen floors above the East Eighties. I am here for divorce counseling. That is, I have come uptown by subway to an office marooned in the sky for help in trying to end my marriage. Marina has left me. She is pregnant with my child. She's left me for another man — the Nominee — and was convinced, at first, that the baby belonged to him. Genetic testing has proved otherwise. My likely paternity has not weakened her resolve to leave me; in fact, she is planning a beach vacation in Italy soon for her, the Nominee, and my unborn son. They are going to Puglia. When I tell her that she has no right to take him — we know that it is a "him," thanks to ultrasound — and accuse her of being completely irresponsible and acting contrary to nature, she gets angry and yells that she can do whatever she wants with her own life. "We're going to the beach," she tells me. "It's the last chance I'll have to take a real vacation before the baby comes and I deserve it!" After conversations like this I can never tell whether she is crazy, or if I am, or if neither one of us has gone insane and, instead, the world is a far, far stranger place than I can fathom.

Did I mention that Marina is refusing to give me a divorce? Or that her mother—my mother-in-law—is dying of cancer? One more thing: we have been married for a little over a year, separated for half of that time, and probably should have called off our wedding in April after I came home from Frankfurt and fell into a guilt spiral for two months before I finally made my confession.

I'm a monster.

You're not a monster.

But I am. I'm a monster.

Once a week I wait for the body-snatched version of my wife to show up in a patch of gravel outside the tower where Dr. Mordechai keeps an office. Marina is late for every appointment; it seems like she's late for everything and always has been. But now she is "I don't care" late. "Go ahead and compel me with a lawyer" late. I show up early anyway, hoping, by some trick of timing, to catch sight of her before she's changed into the hardened, unreachable version of herself who would end our marriage so soon, choose to raise our son with someone else, and—more urgently—carry him in her womb to a secluded beach in southern Italy and make him party to their escape from reason and natural law. I am trying to convince her to call off the trip. It fills me with rage every time I think about it, and I think about it so often, combined with Marina's claim that she's not "ready" to give me a divorce, that I feel weightless and hollowed out. Sleep is no escape—my dreams hold me captive to long episodes of NC-17 violence that make me gasp when I remember them in the morning, if I remember them at all. Bloody knives are brandished, disemboweled animals appear, I am always running from some new and mortal danger. Of course, the underlying wound, the furnace of my anger and the cause of my living nightmare, is the fact that Marina won't snap out of it and try to reconcile now that she knows we are going to have a child. I want her back. I want us to be together as a family. I know this in my heart, and I say it in our sessions, but it doesn't change anything.

I have an ally, I believe, in Dr. Mordechai, a blunt and slow-moving analyst from Israel who specializes, we've been told, in treating couples in crisis. I am not particularly fond of Dr. Mordechai, in part because of the credit card machine he's pointed out to us at the close of every session, but mostly because he seems like an asshole—the kind of asshole, moreover, who's convinced of his ethical superiority. He yawns behind a hand and checks the clock on the wall once our sessions begin, comfortably enthroned in his recliner while we face him, on wheels, in mismatched office chairs from Staples. That is, once Marina has bothered to show up, without apologizing, trailing bags and scarves and gum wrappers. I wait for her out on the street first, watching the residents exit from the high-rise and hail a cab with the automatic gesture that only exists, in such effortless and entitled form, in certain neighborhoods of Manhattan. *Can they know?* I ask myself, in full awareness that no one on that dreary corner of the Upper East Side, save Dr. Mordechai, and maybe not even Dr. Mordechai, has any idea of the medieval torture rack that life has stretched me out on. I check my phone for texts: nothing. I thumb out a quick "Are you close?" and send it to Marina's number. Again, nothing. The wall of taxis surging down the avenue, the old ladies with their lonely shopping carts, the delivery trucks with their shrink-wrapped pallets of boxes—everything that keeps on going as if nothing has changed is an outrage to me. When I can't take waiting for Marina outside any longer, I walk into the lobby of the high-rise and sign in at the desk.

"Dr. Mordechai," I tell the doorman.

"Sixteen," he says without looking up from his paper. He's in full uniform, a deep navy suit with brass buttons and maroon trim. His reading is arrayed on the desk: the *Post*, the *Daily News*, the *New York Times*, the *Wall Street Journal*. If the world were made up of career doormen from Manhattan, the newspaper business would still be booming.

"My wife should be here in a second," I say.

He licks a finger and flips a page of newsprint. "Right."

Does he know? I ask myself on the way to the elevator. *Can he tell?*

No. While it feels like my troubles follow me wherever I go, as material as Pig-Pen's dirty cloud, they are invisible to everyone else.

Dr. Mordechai's high-rise is so badly constructed that phantom air currents whistle down the hallways on the upper floors. It's like being in the wilderness, except with industrial carpeting, drop ceilings, and fluorescent lights. The doors inside his office suite are hard to pry open thanks to the suction force of the wind; once you win the struggle and fight your way through a doorway, the knob flies out of your hand and the door slams open against the drywall. I sit in the waiting room and listen to the building's weather. Dr. Mordechai shares his office with another psycho-therapist whom I've never seen, but I can hear his voice murmuring behind a door. I check for texts: still nothing. I punch in "Waiting room" and flip my phone shut. The framed prints on the walls, the wrinkled copies of the *New Yorker* magazine, the arrangements of silk flowers are supposed to put my mind at ease, make me feel like I'm somewhere safe and comforting and institutionally homelike instead of dangling over the abyss with just my wallet and a working cell phone to prove that I can still function in human society.

Finally, a text message. "Ten minutes. Trains suck."

I am punching out my reply when Dr. Mordechai, impervious to the currents, throws his door open and stands there looking at me. He wears the fussy academic garb of his trade, but still he looks like a pickle barrel. I have heard from the people who referred us that Dr. Mordechai was once a promising soccer player, and I have trouble believing this.

"Just you?" he asks.

"She's running late," I tell him. And then I do something that I can't believe as soon as it's happened: I apologize. For the woman who left me. For the woman who's keeping *me* waiting. I am in that deep. Oh, I am in need of rescue. "Sorry."

"Come in anyway," he says, and heads into his office. I follow, smelling the remnants of a tuna melt as I cross the threshold. The door slams shut behind me under its own power.

We might have been a doomed combination from the start, the three of us, given my daze of incomprehension and the freshness of my wounds, Marina's chronic lateness and her stubborn refusal to do anything in Dr. Mordechai's office but argue for her right to do damage to our lives no matter how little sense it made to me. Dr. Mordechai, for his part, kept us methodically focused, from the comfort of his recliner, on all that was most irrational, hurtful, and beyond our understanding, let alone our ability to control. He enjoyed his work as our puppet master, and he embraced his newfound role as executive producer of the sad little reality experiment we were waging.

Here is how a typical session went, in all of its raw, unfiltered glory:

B.: You've totally abandoned me.

Dr. M.: Tell it to her. She's here now.

B. (*swiveling chair to face Marina*): You've abandoned me. I feel abandoned.

Dr. M.: You mean that's all? What about the baby?

B.: What about the baby?

Dr. M.: How it makes you feel. Tell her.

B.: First you abandon me, and then you take my baby away before he's even born! I can't watch him grow. I can't feel him kick. I can't read to him in the womb. None of the things that a father gets to enjoy before a baby's born, I get to do. You've stolen that whole experience from me. I can't read to him! He doesn't know his own father's voice!

Dr. M.: Respond to that. I can see you're uncomfortable.

M. (*legs up on her chair, chin raised defiantly*): You abandoned me first.

B.: I abandoned you? How?

Dr. M.: How did he abandon you?

M.: You abandoned me by cheating.

B.: But I told you about it. I couldn't handle the lie of not telling you. I asked you to forgive me. You said you did.

M.: I know that and I tried! I tried to forgive you!

Dr. M. (*with a yawn*): But what?

M. (*in tears*): I couldn't do it! It hurt too much! It just hurt, okay?

B.: I forgave you for cheating on me! It's not that hard. It feels pretty fucking great as a matter of fact.

M. (*with sarcasm*): I guess you're just a bigger person than I am . . .

(*A pause. Dr. M. wipes his glasses clean on a shirttail. He's waiting for me to go on.*)

B.: Why did you marry me then? We made a vow in front of our family and all our friends. We got *married*. We had a *wedding*.

M.: I know we had a wedding! It was at *my* godmother's house! My mother played the piano and now she's dying! So don't pretend you're the only one who took our wedding vows seriously! I did too!

B.: You left me six months later!

M.: You're the one who wants a divorce! I don't!

B.: You're living with someone else! In our apartment! He's sleeping in our bed! Do you have any idea what that feels like?

Dr. M. (*perking up*): What does it feel like?

M.: I can't take it anymore! Don't tell me what it feels like! Don't say it! (*The tears slide down her face.*) Why are you both torturing me?

It was so primitive in Dr. Mordechai's office, so instinct-driven and close to the limits of what we could endure, that I wondered, while it was happening, if we were doing ourselves irreparable harm. Marina was like a dying star. A supergiant in an office chair. Something in her had cleaved wide open, and she was throwing off sparks. All around her, in the words of Virginia Woolf, there was "a vast upheaval of matter." She had *power*. It turned me on. I still loved her, but she was determined to go—in her own way, at her own time, without making amends or allowances for what I wanted, what I needed . . . I kept coming back, and so did Marina. We meted out our punishments well and took them even better. Dr. Mordechai was satisfied with the progress we were making and he started giving us little pep talks from his recliner when it was time to leave. I finally caught a glimpse of the athlete he might have been one day when he bounced up from his seat to take my outstretched credit card, flew past Marina in her chair (sobbing) to swipe another $225 onto my MasterCard, and rocked on the balls of his feet while he waited for an approval. After I'd signed and Dr. Mordechai had ushered us out through the waiting room and we started, into a headwind, down the corridor to the elevators, Marina collapsed into a ball on the carpet and lay there writhing and gasping for air. I knelt over her and put my hands on her heaving body. It was the first time I'd touched her in ages. She felt hotter and softer than before, bonier in a few places, but mostly she felt the same—like my wife. I missed her. Back to the scene:

"I'm a monster!" she wails.

"You're not a monster," I say.

"But I am! I'm a monster!"

"That's not true," I insist.

"It is! I'm a monster . . ."

"No, it isn't."

She is coming apart. The wind is whistling around us. I want to put her back together. I remember thinking that: *I want to put her back together*. I am not angry. I take no pleasure in her suffering. I didn't want revenge, and I still don't. Why does life bring us to these places? To know a pain so vast it's like a wilderness? To bring wisdom? I have been over it a hundred times and maybe more and I see no reason for what happened in the corridor that day, no fault great enough to explain what I was doing there with Marina. What we were doing there. I felt responsible. I did. I wanted her to come around so we could reconcile. I thought I owed her whatever I was capable of to make that happen, even if it was just a small, sustaining platitude. *You're not a monster.* But there was something else happening too, and it's harder for me to account for and to name. I've been here before. I remember kneeling in the corridor over Marina, feeling her radiate her sick heat, and having that thought. *I've been here before, and I know just what to do.*

A Disturbance of Memory at
the Brooklyn Flea

ELIZA IS ON TO ME. At least I think she is. I can't be sure, but I do know that she is getting curious about what I've been working on behind the door to Primo's room. I have been waking up early, before sunrise whenever I can, and making coffee in the dark while her cat head-butts my shins and yowls for food. I wait for the espresso to finish bubbling up from its chamber into the top of my coffeepot, wait for the pot to clear its throat and start hissing steam, then I pour myself enough caffeinated nectar to carry me to first light and I pick up this notebook where I left off. We have eleven windows in our apartment. This had been one of its selling points when the realtor walked us through last spring. He had warned us in the elevator that the place was in bad, bad shape; the previous tenants had kept pit bulls, maybe there had been a breeding operation, who knew. They had recently been evicted after twenty years, and the landlord's building crew was patching the walls, putting in a new kitchen, two new bathrooms. Everything would get a fresh coat of paint. I could smell the apartment from down the hall—the reek of dog and damp and rodents under the sink. The door was wide open. Eliza followed the realtor in first, and I saw her go electric. There were gouges in the walls. All the appliances had been ripped out. The smell leaking out of one of the bedrooms was so foul it made me feel lightheaded. "Do you see the windows?" Eliza said to me as we followed the realtor down the hall. She turned to me and gripped my arm. "*Do you see them?*"

I often think of this early in the morning, while Eliza is still asleep, and I look up from these pages to watch the sunrise fill our windows. We are on the sixth floor of our building, high enough to give a panoramic view of Brooklyn's rooftops and its water towers and its church spires falling into ink-black silhouette as the sky grows blue; the streetlights stitching their way out to Bushwick in the east and, farther on, the leafy fringe of Queens; acres of apartments tumbling up the hill to Prospect Park. We are gentrifiers. I know: the term is usually reserved for the moneyed. Judging by the mail that still arrives, the last tenant was an active member of the International Brotherhood of Electrical Workers Local Union No. 3, which means his income likely dwarves mine at the moment. If he's working, that is. Debt seems to be dogging his trail too; we've been getting the same mailers about consolidation programs, fake telegrams from collection agencies marked "urgent" and "personal." The kind of law firm that specializes in shaking down the divorced, the unemployed, the uninsured, the debt-ridden. I try my best to get the mail before Eliza does every day and prune out the ugly, anything to not remind her of how far I need to come before we're safe, before we can enjoy the freedom — I love the word F. Scott Fitzgerald used for being flush: "toploftiness" — that comes from being able to spend without worry.

I can look the part. We both do. Especially Eliza. Our neighborhood, Clinton Hill, has suddenly become a fashionable place to live, and every Saturday while the weather is still warm we head out to a flea market — the Brooklyn Flea — that takes over the running track and handball courts behind a Catholic high school. It's like no flea market that I was ever dragged to as a child: there are antique Oriental rugs, reclaimed pharmacy cabinets, organic cotton T-shirts silk-screened with natural and sustainable vegetable dyes, racks of vintage designer dresses that Eliza can call out by name and decade. There is artisanal ice cream, handmade *pupusas*, *porchetta* sandwiches sliced with a stoner's "There you go, dude," and a wood-burning oven for blisteringly hot margherita pizzas. You can have a lobster roll, browse picture frames made from distressed lumber shipped from West Africa, buy a Pendleton blanket that looks like it just came off work at a photo shoot. It does not feel like real life at the Flea; it is a bazaar with velvet ropes outside, a marketplace for just the cool kids.

"Where's all the junk?" I ask Eliza as we wander through the stalls, holding hands. "Did they forget to bring it? You know, the Crock-Pot that doesn't work and the depressing sneakers." It is a scene: visitors from Europe and Latin America snap pictures on their iPhones; roommates in aviator sunglasses pass us in gaggles of two and three; other Brooklyn homesteaders like us, either pushing strollers or trailing a toddler or two, stare beleagueredly out from their lives and take our measure — are we ahead of them or behind? did they buy more stuff? are we losing or winning? — before their eyes go blank and they pretend that this isn't what they were just doing.

"Maybe we should split up," Eliza says, starting to get that faraway bargain hunter's look. Her body stiffens; she is on the alert for vintage. "I want to check a few things."

Her hand is warm in mine. It is a perfect blue fall day. It feels like we are at the epicenter of fabulous, and I can hardly believe my luck. The asphalt shimmers. *Outside the fence,* I think, *I am alone again. I am broke. I am almost forty-two. In here I've got Eliza. I don't want to leave.*

75

"I'm kind of getting hungry," I say out loud.

"Me too."

"Why don't I get in line for the *pupusas*," I suggest.

"Really?"

"It's a big sacrifice, I know."

"That would be awesome," she says.

"How's jalapeño and cheese?"

"Yum."

"See you by the food," I tell her, and we part ways.

I want you to stay.

I know you can't wait forever.

I made you a promise.

I want to keep it.

I can pay for the *pupusas* this time, two to share with all the fixings. I've been freelancing at a shelter magazine off and on, so I have at least a little pocket money. I order us two lemonades to round out the feast. It hasn't always gone this way when we've come to the Flea, and I can see relief in Eliza's face when she finds me with lunch already paid for and waiting. We eat our *pupusas* on the concrete steps where people sit and take a breather from their shopping. We pass the Styrofoam container back and forth and share our *pupusas* with a single fork, squinting into the autumn sun. The Bicycle People are all here, straddling their rides outside the fence and walking the booths with their helmets on; the Dog People are here too, chatting and crouching to scratch any warm belly offered up to them, with their royal breeds in backpacks or tucked into the crook of an arm. We are We People. The couples who don't bicker in public yet and look miserable with their burdens. I often joke with Eliza that the only way to tell that Primo is not her biological child, when we're all together, is by how often we have our arms around each other, or steal a quick kiss when he's off playing.

We just blew your cover, I warn her at the playground. *Now all the mothers know that you're the girlfriend.*

Really? She swivels her head around. *They can tell?*

Take note. The playground is PDA-free.

You're right, she says. *It is!*

Kind of sad, isn't it?

"So I've got a question for you," she says.

"Go ahead."

We've finished eating our *pupusas* and we're sitting in the sun. It is starting to get chilly; the afternoon is here. Another few degrees, and Eliza might be leaving with a new cardigan. There is also the question of a pair of Gucci loafers that she's willing to go as high as $35 for — if they haven't been snatched up by someone else already.

"It might be too early," she goes on, "but how would you feel about showing me some of your pages?"

The question sinks in. I choke on my lemonade. The drink spews out of the straw and onto my sweater. I stare at the mess for a second and then start dabbing at it with a napkin.

"Christ."

"Sorry, baby."

"You ambushed me," I say.

I am supposed to be writing a novel. I want to be writing a novel. I have notes on the main characters saved on my desktop, scenes sketched out on blank pages in the books stacked at my bedside and others that I've thumbed out on my Slab. I even have a working title: *The Upper Room.* I know that will change, but it doesn't bother me. Still: all I'm able to think about whenever I sit down to write is being broke, and looking for a job, and how much I miss my son, and paying off my miserable debts, and trying to build a new life with Eliza out of the fortune that I do have: a stack of notebooks, some small change.

"I know you're working hard," she says.

"I am." I finish cleaning up the lemonade and ball up the soggy napkin. "I've seen a lot of sunrises in Primo's room lately. Sunrise Over Monster Trucks."

She pokes a little deeper, cheerfully. "Is it going well?"

"Sure."

"How well?"

"Well, I think."

She is deflating. I don't like disappointing her. I hate it.

"It's not that I don't want you to read it," I say. "Really."

Now she is deflated. "Okay."

"What?"

The schoolyard is starting to echo. Suddenly, it is new cardigan weather. She looks at me with the same intensity that hooked me when we met, in a bookstore. (I know, it's a little much. Sometimes I think we should have gone across the street to the butcher shop and talked instead, in front of the rosy cuts of meat laid out behind the meat counter, our feet slippery on the sawdust. It was closed, though, and that's how we met: at a reading.) It's a look that I'm familiar with now and have had some time to ponder. It *expects* things. It's a look that dares you to live up to it. I took the dare. I am better for it.

"I'm trying not to worry."

"I know you are," I say.

"But it's hard."

She looks out over the Flea. It is past its peak for the day. It is middle-aged. It has turned; an emptiness has started trickling in from outside, beyond the fences. I can always tell when Eliza is doing her math. At least I think I can. *Days left to 40 + x (privately defined grace period) / y (personal sense of urgency) – z (realization that I will be a fatal drag to any mortgage application).* She is trying to make the numbers work. She is running the equation in her head, again and again.

"We're not talking about the book anymore," I say. "Are we?"

It takes a while for her to answer.

I went to see the ring today. The one I want to give Eliza. It is under glass at the counter of a boutique I like to call Plaid Flannel & English Leather. She chose it herself: I am not stupid enough to pick out an engagement ring for a former features editor at a fashion magazine and the daughter of an interior decorator, even if Eliza does spend most of her days now sitting cross-legged on the couch in her workout clothes, either reading other people's books to review or writing a novel of her own. "I know we can't afford it now," she said the first time she showed it to me. "But maybe when you finish your novel . . ." It is a black diamond, a stone I have never seen before — the color of smoke and embers, so clear it could be made of water. It is like a piece of a storm cloud cut into an oval, shined until it glitters, and set into a bed of gold. I am known at the boutique by now. It is a sign of the times, just like the Brooklyn Flea, that you can walk into the door of an old French dry cleaner between a Laundromat and a bodega, say a few words to the right hipster, and the next thing you know, you are holding a ring worth many thousands of dollars up to the light and discussing its virtues with someone who looks like she's either a grad student or in the band Arcade Fire. This is not the first time I've seen a copy of *The Žižek Reader* splayed open next to a cash register.

"It's a one-of-a-kind piece," the shopgirl in horn-rimmed glasses says.

"I can see that." I hold the ring by its band and turn it under the light. It is a stone to gaze at and get lost in — I have never had any feelings one way or the other about a diamond, not even the family heirloom from Austro-Hungary that I gave to Marina on a subway platform, but this one is different. It is a reflecting pool. It is liquid mercury. It is aurora borealis. It is wonder distilled. And I can't afford it: not even close. Still I am here, making a pilgrimage.

"The stone was cut in Jaipur."

"Where's that?" I say.

"Rajasthan."

"It's so rad."

We have been joined at the counter by another employee with horn-rimmed glasses and wearing plaid flannel, this one with a beard. Aside from the three of us, the store is empty.

"What's the carat count?" Plaid Flannel #2 asks.

"The stone, you mean?"

"Yeah."

"I think nine," Plaid Flannel #1 says. "Yeah, nine."

"That's healthy."

"I just want to keep staring," I say.

"It's so, like, minimal." Plaid Flannel #2 again.

If I can put down a credit card and walk out of the store with that ring, it will mean that I am free of debt, that I have paid for all the history that brought me here. That I have money in my pocket. That I still have Eliza. That I have kept my promise and she is still here.

Plaid Flannel #1 sighs.

"What?" Plaid Flannel #2 asks.

"The girl you buy this for," she says to me, still gazing into the stone, "is going to be so fucking happy."

How did I get here?

I keep asking myself the same questions, early in the mornings, while the far-off yawn of the city waking up grows louder, the rumbling starts, the airplanes rise and fall in the sky with jet engines shrieking. While the light fills Primo's room and I am faced with another day without him, another twenty-four-hour marathon of uncertainty.

Symmetry. Too much symmetry.

Too Good to Be True

THERE'S A MEMORY I have, the earliest on the playlist that's determined who I am. It's always had a special power over me, even if I've never understood why that is, or what the memory means. When I was younger — still a child — and much closer to the time when it takes place, the memory, as incomplete as it was, used to bring on a numb, abstracted feeling that would almost paralyze me, the fear that I wasn't in control of my own life, my own destiny. I would lie awake in the middle of the night and replay the memory in my head until I felt connected to a pain so deep and old and mysterious and not of my own making that I couldn't begin to name it aloud, let alone chase it away. Later, as I got older, I learned to disarm the memory of its power by telling it aloud to the amazement of friends, tease it out long or slow depending on my audience, use their laughter as a kind of Novocain.

It begins with a glimpse of my family intact. My first family, the original one. Before my parents went off to find themselves in other lives, settled down with the second parents I have known for decades now. It's the one memory I have of all of us living under the same roof: my mother, my father, my brother, my twin sister, me. My mother is lying on the couch. There is something wrong with her, but I don't know what it is. She doesn't want to get up. She doesn't want to move. She doesn't want to do anything. My father is on the phone with her doctor in the kitchen. They are hollering back and forth to each other between the rooms. The doctor wants her to go to the hospital, but she doesn't want to go. I don't want her to go. But she has to. My father yells, "You don't have any choice!" I can see sunlight in this memory. I can see my father standing in the kitchen, holding the black receiver to his ear, and I can see my mother lying on the couch. But that's all. The memory stops.

Next, we are together, without my father, at a place that is like a hospital, but not a hospital. It has a name: Freedom to Be. There is a big, wide parking lot with traffic cones where we sometimes play. There are buildings with tall staircases that we like to climb, trees and grass and hedges and stone walls. It is summertime, and the days are hot. We sleep and eat together in one building—big group meals where everyone has a different job. My brother, sister, and I pitch in and help. Most of the adults don't pay attention to us and stay in little groups instead, tapping cigarettes on the table before they light them. I have a favorite adult who always talks to me: his name is Jimmy Stone. In my memory, Jimmy Stone is younger than the rest of the adults; he is almost one of us. He wears a white T-shirt every day and a baggy pair of chinos. A beat-up pair of tennis sneakers. He lifts me high in the air when he sees me in the place we have dinner and then I laugh when I say his name out loud. His name is funny. There is something wrong with Jimmy Stone, just like there is something wrong with my mother, but it doesn't bother me. He's my friend. That's what he says:

"Friends, right?"

"Friends," I say.

"Good," he tells me. "I need one."

In the day, and sometimes at night too, our mother is away in group. When she's in group, there is always someone to take care of us. A few of them are staff, which is special; they ask a lot of questions. They watch us playing with one another. They ask us to draw things and use building blocks. They tell us to move the blocks between different boxes and to keep them "organized." My brother hates doing any of the things they ask and argues with the adults a lot, so they usually end up taking him off by himself for long talks. My sister and I are better at doing what we're told when our mother is away in group, although sometimes she misses our mother and she cries. I try to make her feel better. She is my twin sister. I know her face even better than my own. I try.

One day, while our mother is in group, they bring us to the room where they watch us playing and sit us down. I have no memory of what they say to us. But for each of us they have a sign: my brother's sign says MR. KNOW-IT-ALL, my sister's sign says CRYBABY, and mine says TOO GOOD TO BE TRUE. The signs are hand-lettered on white cardboard. They punch holes in the corners and tie a piece of string to each so we can wear the signs around our necks. That is our job: to wear signs. We do what we're told and put them on. We go outside. I have a vague memory of playing under a tree with my sister, and I don't like her sign. Not one bit. I tell her that she's not a crybaby and she doesn't have to worry. At lunch, Jimmy Stone gets upset when he sees me at the table wearing my TOO GOOD TO BE TRUE sign. He won't look anyone in the eye, including me. He doesn't talk. I eat in silence too. After we're done and the adults are smoking cigarettes over in the lounge, I can see him talking with the staff person who made us wear the signs. He is trying to keep his cool. He points in my direction and turns an incredible shade of red. Jimmy Stone. My friend. Jimmy Stone. The staff person puts a hand on Jimmy Stone's shoulder to try to calm him down. He rips himself away and goes over to a corner, where he smokes a cigarette on the couch and keeps on punching the cushions, over and over. It's the last image I have of him in my mind, and I don't know if it's real or if I dreamed it up. I go out into the sunlight and the grass again, still wearing my TOO GOOD TO BE TRUE sign. I wear it for the rest of the day, and I don't cry.

My twin sister and I are three. My brother is seven. We are far away from home. We miss our father. Sometimes we get scared. There is something wrong with our mother that has brought us to this place, but we don't know what it's called.

Let's start with what I do know. It was 1972. My parents had been married for seven years and they were in the middle of splitting up. In the first glimpse from that time, my father—picture a brooding Greek beatnik in a uniform of dungarees, a navy-blue T-shirt, and sandals, potbellied from lentils and with a beard down to his solar plexus chakra—is trying to admit my mother to the hospital. She is much too skinny in the pictures that survive from that time, but still my mother is an aquiline beauty with swimming black eyes, fond of leather Nehru jackets, big wooden hoop earrings, and colorful silk headscarves. Despite dropping out of college in her first semester when she found out that she was pregnant with my brother, she has taught herself the early programming language COBOL and works nights to earn money at a local fish-processing plant. She is a programmer instead of packing haddock and scrod for the supermarket freezer with the other women. She is twenty-six and an orphan, having survived the death of her mother from misdiagnosed lupus when she was eighteen and her father's suicide just two years later, from a gunshot to the head. She was in the house when it happened, when the gun went off in his closet. My grandfather's death certificate

reads: "Suicide — shotgun wound, left side of face below ear."
The time of death is listed as "about" 9:00 A.M. on March 22,
1966. The shotgun part is wrong; he did it much more neatly,
with a .22 rifle. My grandfather was an acoustic engineer, so
sound and how it traveled was an area of research he knew well.
He knew the closet would dampen the sound of the rifle shot
when he pulled the trigger, knew the .22 was the right weapon for
the job. No one heard the report upstairs. They discovered him
later, when he didn't appear before going to work. He died alone
on his closet floor dressed in his pajamas, his bathrobe, and a
pair of slippers. It was an event of such magnitude, my grandfather's suicide, that it threatened to take my mother along with
it, swallow up the rest of us too. No one ever talked about my
grandfather's suicide when I was growing up, but I could feel its
undertow beneath our lives. I can still feel it tugging at my heels
and dragging on my heart, even as I write this.

I'd always assumed that the second part of the memory, the
one involving the signs we had to wear, was a classic example of
early childhood therapy gone wrong. It was the 1970s. There was
a lot of bad, faddish therapy around: encounter groups, primal
screaming, all-night Gestalt therapy marathons run by chain-
smoking gurus in church basements and school auditoriums. My
parents tried to avoid the worst of it, but they had adopted the
"simple living, high thinking" ethic of the 1960s as a way of life,
and for them, there was no higher thinking than psychoanalytic
theory, no road to being conscious and engaged in the battles
of their time that didn't involve being in psychotherapy of some
kind. They had both read Norman O. Brown's *Life Against
Death*, with its dire warnings: "Freud was right in positing a
death instinct," Brown writes, "and the development of weapons
of destruction makes our present dilemma plain: we either come
to terms with our unconscious instincts and drives — with life

and with death—or else we surely die." We were dragged along to therapy the same way that other kids are brought to church. It was our ritual when we were young. We got used to killing time together in waiting rooms, where we were told to play or read our comic books despite the muffled drama going on behind the office door; sometimes one of the therapists would call us in to ask us questions much too slowly, encourage us to tattle on one another, and finish by letting us whale on each other with foam clubs they called Batacas. To be fair, my brother usually started to whale on me no matter where we were or who was watching, so the Batacas were an improvement. They landed softly, with an appealing bounce, and left no marks. I'm not sure I can say the same about my TOO GOOD TO BE TRUE sign.

Traditional psychiatry had failed my mother. She wanted to be happy. She wanted to be free. In the summer of 1972, she found herself in a terrible bind: she needed treatment for her depression, but another hospitalization would mean that she was separated from us. She would risk losing custody, or even having us taken away by the state. The only alternative was an experimental residential treatment program—this was Freedom to Be—run by a practice where she had been doing group therapy. We would all be treated at the same time, mother and children. It was a group home "situation" modeled after successful drug treatment programs, meaning that residents shared chores and responsibilities, everyone participated in daily therapy sessions, and group leaders were always on hand to monitor residents and police their interactions. The goal was to break down the residents' defenses in order to liberate the true, authentic selves buried inside, beneath the roles we adopt in society—starting with our role within the family. Wilhelm Reich, the most radical figure to come out of Freud's Vienna, believed that all of us develop defenses that he called "character armor" to protect ourselves from blows from the outside world and from within. This armor serves a purpose, but it ultimately becomes a prison. Shatter the patient's character armor, the theory went, and the unconscious will be liberated. It started with breaking down the rational control mechanisms, or what Freud called the superego. "Lose your mind," wrote Fritz Perls, the founder of the Gestalt therapy method, "and come to your senses."

The program lasted all summer, and conflict was the norm. My father was called in for special sessions known as "psycho-dramas" where he was forced to sit and listen while my mother confronted him in front of the group for his failings as a husband, which were numerous, and for his role in enabling her depression. These sessions were videotaped by the staff for later replay, and they were stage-managed for maximum discomfort. After a discouraging start, my mother took to this form of treatment well and started to feel stronger, liberated, more confident. In short: she started to get better. I don't know at what point they hung the signs on us; it must have been after they'd observed us together long enough to identify roles they believed were accurate, or at least true enough to sting. How could they not sting, when we were forced into wearing our diagnoses around our necks like the scarlet letter *A* and face the judgment of our colony full of dropouts, misfits, and casualties?

If you have noticed running through these pages a certain, well, mistrust of mental health professionals, it should be clear now why that is. I was subjected to character analysis at the age of three, made to watch the same thing happen to my brother and my sister, and punished, in the end, for trying to be better than I was — for *trying too hard to be good* at the same time my family was coming apart. What if I was just good? What if I didn't want my mother to be so unhappy? My father to be so angry all the time? Or my sister to burst into tears every time she thought a fight was about to start? What if my brother tried to pretend he knew everything in the world to protect himself from what he couldn't control? Would that be such a bad thing? I was rehashing all this again the other night while I read *The Seven Storey Mountain* in bed and I found this passage about Freud from Merton's student years in Cambridge:

> Day after day I read Freud, thinking myself to be very enlightened and scientific when, as a matter of fact, I was about as scientific as an old woman secretly poring over books about occultism, trying to tell her own fortune, and learning how to dope out the future from the lines in the palm of her hand. I don't know if I ever got very close to needing a padded cell: but if I had gone crazy, I think psychoanalysis would have been the one thing chiefly responsible for it.

I used to fantasize about the lawsuit I would file against the ponytailed sign-hangers who treated us that summer for endangering our welfare and searing an experience so clearly wrong and clinically misguided into our memories, even if it's turned out to be more of a curiosity—an indictment of a time and place—than a shattering event. I imagined going to law school, honing my chops on some smaller cases, strictly pro bono, then coming after the freaks behind Freedom to Be for seven figures, maybe eight, in a storm of outraged publicity. I wanted to make them suffer public humiliation just like we had, and, at the same time, I could carry the mantle of justice high, like Atticus Finch.

Sadly, there were several problems with this fantasy, the most serious being that I would have had to go to law school. Beyond that, I had another issue: who could I serve with papers? By the time I was dreaming of a show trial in the civil courts of Massachusetts, the practice had disbanded, the founding ponytail had run into some issues involving female patients and the use of sex surrogates in "therapy," and the rest of the group had drifted off into other lives, different states. My aunt remembers running into a therapist from the group years later (she also stayed at Freedom to Be that summer), and he reported that he had left psychotherapy and had changed his name to Jeremiah—just Jeremiah. I would have changed my name to an untraceable alias too, given how badly they mishandled the three small children in their care. If they had hung those signs on us in any other decade than the 1970s, I expect that my lawsuit would have been more than an idle daydream. They would have paid for their trespasses, every one of them.

Still, I have to admit something. And it's hard for me to do. As much as the signs we had to wear at Freedom to Be were a symbol of all that was not free in their practice, all that was coercive, cruel, and wrongheaded, here's the thing: they nailed us. On that drab and faraway campus off the highway, in the common rooms and in the dangerous privacy of stifling summer offices, the therapist team in charge of our punishment practiced a spooky, clairvoyant art. They saw me. They saw all three of us. They knew how I would turn out. Could it be that a diagnosis scrawled in Magic Marker all those years ago by an anonymous Dr. Feelbad gives the explanation for how I wandered so far off track in life? Have I found my way back to that original condition, powerless and scared, in some kind of autosuggestive trance? If I am lost and broke because I have tried to be TOO GOOD TO BE TRUE too often, will being TRUE instead reverse the losing trend and set me free? Will my son find his own way, immune to my mistakes, or am I only scattering a trail so that he will follow me?

Let's go back to the carpeted wind tunnel in Dr. Mordechai's shabby high-rise. As I wrote a little earlier: my ex-wife has dropped to the floor on our way to the elevator banks and is writhing in the corridor. While I kneel over her on the carpet, trying to soothe her for reasons that I can't even begin to fathom, she starts wailing, "I'm a monster." I could tell her that she is. I could say, *You know what? You are a monster. You haven't always been a monster, but now you are. Yes, I cheated on you. Yes, we took a shortcut and got married when we should have been figuring out if we belonged together at all. But that's no excuse for breaking our vows and kidnapping my unborn child and taking him on a romantic trip to Puglia with the Nominee. That's the kind of thing a monster does. That monsters do. You are a monster, Marina, and I didn't make you.* It won't fix anything. It won't make our pregnancy-and-separation drama any more understandable, or less extreme. It won't undo any of the damage we've done, or restore the broken order of our lives. But if I get up off the ground, where I've knelt to comfort the woman who has left me less than a year into our marriage, who is pregnant with my child and wants to raise him together with her boyfriend, the Nominee, without giving me a divorce because she "isn't ready"; if I stand up and say it, "You are a monster," turn away and head to the elevator banks and press the down button, then at least I will be honest. I will not be pretending.

Will I be TRUE then?

Will it make a difference?

It takes a lifetime of practice to betray yourself without showing any effort, to be so dream-locked and absent that you say the reverse of what you mean, over and over again, to do the opposite of what is good for you. I cannot recommend this modus operandi to everyone, unless you'd like to fall headlong into insolvency (mine is financial; there are other kinds for other people) and see your worst fears — and more — realized. It wasn't always like this, though. I would be lying if I didn't also admit that being TOO GOOD TO BE TRUE has had its advantages. It served me well for a long time, until it didn't anymore. What began as a coping mechanism for dealing with parents who were busy finding themselves and seeking happiness when I was young would only later evolve into a kind of spell — the enchantment I am trying to awake from now. I hope it is working. I am touching every charm I have, resorting to every superstition, setting alarms all over the apartment. *Wake up*, I tell myself. *Wake up!* I have even, if you remember, enlisted God's help by banging on the doors of his empty house just down the block. But the past keeps calling me back: In my ears, I hear the distant putter of a blue VW Bug, paler than the sky and faded from the elements, from the wet New England sun. My father is at the wheel. I am in the backseat, tossed against my sister with every careening turn. My brother sits in front with his elbow hanging out the window, preteen style. It is one of our regular weekend visits to see my father in Gloucester, the town where he was born, and we have been herded into the car for errands. My father is a Marxist revolution of one, an erratic driver with a manifesto for every billboard; no A/C in the summer, barely any heat in winter; a single working seat belt (for him); and a top speed on his best days of 53 mph.

Picture our caravan rolling to a stop in the parking lot of the local A&P. My father yanks the emergency brake and lets the car die with a shudder. We sit in the parking space for a moment while he pulls out his wallet and counts the bills inside. There is never much money. That we all know. We are not supposed to care about money, not supposed to want more. If we did, that would make us like Republicans and Pigs. We are not like the other families in the parking lot with their fresh barber cuts, collared shirts, and lace-up shoes, their station wagons with fake wood siding. Our hair is longer and wilder, our clothing homemade or hand-me-down — except for our Toughskins from Sears. We wear matching smocks on school picture day that my mother has embroidered by hand with rainbows, starfish, seaweed, and kelp. For the trip to the supermarket, we are wearing cutoffs, sandals. My father's beard is at its bushiest, and he is so dark from foraging for arrowheads at the beach all summer long that a stranger recently raised a fist in the air and flashed the Black Power symbol at him from a passing car. My father has never been so proud. "Like this," he says when he reenacts it from the driver's seat, thrusting a fist through the open window of his VW as we putter through the streets of Gloucester. We laugh in the backseat wildly. He always makes us laugh . . .

A long, shiny luxury sedan glides past us in search of parking, and my father looks up from his wallet.

"There they go," he says, watching them. "Mr. and Mrs. America."

"Where?" I ask with my face pressed up to the glass. "Where?"

"Ha," my brother says. "You fell for it." He hocks up a quick loogie and leans out the window to spit it out on the asphalt. First, he lets it dangle. Reeling it back in will be next to impossible. Still, he tries.

"Where are they?" my sister asks, pressing into me to peer out the window too. "I didn't see Mr. and Mrs. America."

"Kids," my father says, "it's an expression." He doesn't have a lot of patience for our political naïveté. "What I mean is, they're the perfect American couple with two Cadillacs in the garage and everything you could ever want." He watches them ease into a parking space. "By God! The car's so big it must run on nuclear power."

My brother loses his loogie and drops back into his seat. "It's *Miss* America," he says, wiping his chin dry with a forearm. "There's no such thing as Mrs. America. Or Mr."

"All right," my father says. "All right."

"What about Captain America?" I ask.

"That's a comic book, retard."

"So what?" I tell him.

"*Mrs. America*," he mocks.

"He's making fun of me, Dad," I report.

"Kids," my father warns. "That's enough."

"What do you want," my brother asks me, "a rupture?"

"You can't give me a rupture."

"Oh, I can't?" he asks. "You've got a rupture coming."

"No, I don't."

My sister stares worriedly out the car window. Her braids are coming loose, one of her barrettes is dangling, and she has a deep furrow in the center of her brow.

"*Kids,*" my father warns again. He's about to lose his temper. "That's enough aggression for one day. I mean it. Fighting with each other won't resolve anything." He turns to face my brother. "You're turning a shopping trip into another Vietnam."

We follow my father between the cars on our way into the supermarket. We are in downtown Gloucester, by the waterfront, and we can hear the seagulls crying closer to the docks. A few strays cross the sky high above us, on their own errands. The air smells like ripening fish, like the mud at low tide. We try to keep up with my father, but he is racing ahead. When we are in public, he gets distracted and starts walking too fast, mutters to himself. Sometimes, we have to call out and remind him that we're there: "Dad, slow down!" I watch the other shoppers in their loud plastic clothes stare at my father as he barrels toward them in his Jesus sandals, clutch their overstuffed grocery bags a little tighter. I have been trained to call their polyester clothing "loud" and "plastic," at least among us. I am used to the way strangers stare at my father, and I am used to the way that, after staring at him, they turn and stare at us. Only later will I recognize the look in their eyes for what it is: pity. I don't like being stared at by strangers. I don't like being judged. If I had a choice, I would rather not be seen at all. I would be invisible.

"Peeeter!"

My father doesn't hear his name from the other side of the parking lot, is too deep in thought to notice.

"Peeeeeeter!"

This time he hears it. He stops in his tracks. He's almost at the entrance to the supermarket, right below the sign: a big red dot with an *A* and *P*. Sales posters for canned vegetables, fish sticks, and frozen pies surround him. Cool Whip. All the things that we aren't allowed to have live inside. It feels like an immense injustice. There is a moment in the parking lot before I realize what is about to happen, what my father is about to do, and I want the moment to keep going on, I want it to last all afternoon. But it doesn't. I have been here before, I have felt my heart start pounding in my throat and the world slowing down. I know I can't stop my father. I don't want to see. But I can't turn away.

My father is about to moon someone. In the A&P parking lot.

I should pause for a moment and explain, from the safety of adulthood, that my father had three major styles when it came to mooning. The first and probably the most common type happened in the car, when my father was behind the wheel. Let's call it the Face in the Window. If we were driving through Gloucester and passed a friend from his wilder, artsy crowd, he would sometimes put the car in neutral, crouch up on the seat, yank down his pants, and press his bare ass to the glass. Sometimes he did the same thing when the car was parked, but that version had a lower degree of difficulty. I had seen the Face in the Window from the outside enough times to fear it: the twin mounds of flesh pressed hard against the window; the dark crevice down the center, like a crack in the earth; the beard of pubic hair and dangling ball sack. No one, no matter what his suit of character armor, should have to contemplate the furry pucker of his father's asshole in the window of a car, or anywhere else. It leads to nightmares. It is like seeing your own death. Actually, it's like seeing your own death and staring at your father's asshole at the same time.

His second style of mooning was an offshoot of the first: the Breezeway. This is identical to the Face in the Window, except the car windows are open. It's fresher, more natural. Easier to shrug off, if you happen to catch some collateral.

The third style of mooning is the easiest to employ on the fly: the Quick Drop. This is the moon my father used when he was on foot. It could happen in an instant, at any time. He dropped his pants, threw himself over forward, and reached behind to spread his ass cheeks wide. Without the spread it was still a full-on mooning, but the effect was a little more restrained, more polite.

In front of the A&P, while we look on from a short distance behind, helpless, my father employs the Quick Drop. He unfastens his dungarees, yanks them down, and bends forward to expose his ass cheeks to the sun. Luckily, he's happy to stop there and doesn't add a spread. We are spared a glimpse of the Black Hole all children fear most in the universe, especially sons.

I can hear the gulls, the sound of nearby traffic. It's peaceful. Laughter from my father's friend carries across the parking lot. The doors to the A&P are still. No one comes in or out. And there is my father in all his pale-assed glory, bent over so far that we can see his face between his legs, upside down.

"Fuck you, Peter!" his friend yells.

"Go fuck yourself!" my father yells back, still upside down. His face is turning red. He is grinning wide.

"Right on!"

"Jesus," my brother says. "Dad!" He puts his hands on his knees and starts to laugh. He can barely breathe, he's laughing so hard.

"Dad!" my sister pleads beside me. "Can you *stop*?"

The doors to the A&P start to swing open.

There are people coming out.

Leave behind the drama in the A&P parking lot, spied by gulls circling high in the sky, and rejoin my tattered, unruly family at the apartment in Cambridge, on the ground floor of a creaking two-family Victorian ruin, where we lived most nights of the week with our mother. I remember the single rotary-dial phone that hung on the wall in the front room and the resistance against my finger whenever I carried a chair in from the dining room and stood on top of it to dial, the tufts of horsehair peeking out from holes in the crumbling plaster walls, the box of yoga flash cards my mother kept on a shelf beside her bed and that I sometimes borrowed after school to try to master the lotus position while I took in my daily overdose of afternoon reruns on our portable twelve-inch black-and-white TV.

There is a wooden stash-box on the mantelpiece in the living room that we are not allowed to touch according to the rules, although my brother has already developed an encyclopedic knowledge of the little baggies and the equipment inside: whether it's better to pack a pipe with "shake" or "bud," the relative merits of homegrown dope or Hawaiian. My mother has gone back to school to get a master's degree in social work — later she will get her PhD — so we are usually alone in the house after school. My brother has been put "in charge" in her absence until dinnertime, and he rules those empty hours indifferently, if at all. He is too busy finding trouble in the unsupervised wilderness of our neighborhood, its peeling mansions, pitted brick sidewalks, and fenced-in yards, to bother with my sister and me. Unless he's angry. Then he tracks me down.

"Take this," he says, and throws me one of our Batacas. They are denim, with hard rubber handles. We fight with our Batacas so often that the seams are starting to split and the yellow foam inside is showing. Our battles usually start out painless, but they never end well. If I can escape with just a bloody nose then I will be happy. I will lock myself in the bathroom and sit on the toilet lid with a wad of tissue up my nostril, waiting for my brother to get bored, waiting for him to stop pounding on the door and threatening me with more.

I am on the floor, in my best full lotus, watching *Hogan's Heroes*. My sister is in the next room with two of her best friends, trying to coax her pet hamster, Hamlet, under the blow dryer after giving him a bath. "Hammie!" they squeal. The foam end of the Bataca hits me in the face. It glances off and rolls away on the kitchen floor.

"Stop it," I tell my brother. "You're supposed to leave me alone."

"Fight me," he says. My brother is short for his age and he is angry about it. His Toughskins come from the Husky aisle, and that makes him angry too. He is eleven years old and already he is skipping school, failing to show up for therapy appointments, stretching the truth to my mother and his teachers for the sport of it. He has just been fitted for braces, and that makes him even angrier. Soon he will learn to use them as a weapon, shooting the tiny, aim-able rubber bands from his mouth at will. They pack a sting when they land on bare skin. They leave tiny red welts that look like bug bites.

"I'm not fighting you," I tell him.

He takes a step closer. He starts swinging his Bataca under his arms and over his head like Bruce Lee.

"C'mon, fight me."

"I said I'm not fighting you!"

"Yeah, you are."

He takes a swing at me with his Bataca and I try to block it, but the denim whops me full on in the face. I turn away and put my hands up, but it's no use. He makes a lunge, and the next thing I know he is standing over me, walloping me with his Bataca again and again. I hear ringing in my ears. I see stars. I can hear the girls in the next room calling out to the hamster, who has escaped their grooming session and disappeared into the dark corners of my sister's bedroom.

"Come out, Hammie!"

"Hammie, come back!"

"Hammie," my sister sings, "where are you?"

I am not going to bleed on the kitchen floor and then wipe it from the tiles on my hands and knees with Windex so my mother won't see it when she gets home, so she won't worry. Not this time. Instead I take my punishment balled up on the floor and hope that my brother will tire himself out before it escalates too far, before the elbows and the knees and the fists start flying.

"*Die,*" I hear him grunting with every swing. "*Die . . . Die . . . Die.*"

My mother likes to throw parties, and they are always potluck. She invites her friends from graduate school, and the kitchen fills up with casseroles and baking dishes leaking sour smells: eggplant surprise, cold buckwheat noodles with peanut sauce, lentils and refried beans, veggie stir-fry. My brother plays albums in his room all night, but not before taking a look at what we have for dinner and pronouncing it "grody." I sit on the living-room floor with my soggy paper plate of food, trying to eat as quickly as I can and ignore the adult conversations going on around me.

My mother's friends are nice enough, but they act a little weird around us. They try to "bond" and "communicate." They ask too many questions, just like the therapists we have to see when my brother is "acting out." They dress like they've just been hiking (summer) or cross-country skiing (winter). They laugh too loudly at their jokes, give each other lots of back rubs, don't notice the lumps of potluck dinner nesting in their beards.

"Mmm," my mother's friend Alice says next to me. "I just love tamari dressing on a salad." I know Alice because we've had dinner over at her house before. She has long, straight hair parted in the middle and round glasses. All over her apartment, in frames, she has nude pictures of herself. It's part of her therapy, my mother tells us. I know that Alice has weirdly lopsided breasts, big nipples, and an incredible thicket of black pubic hair underneath her hiking shorts. It makes it hard to look at her while we talk. There is a lot of adult nudity in my life. It is the Golden Age of pubic hair. I walk under a nude portrait of my father painted by his girlfriend every time I climb the stairs of his house. I wonder why they all feel the need to strip down and show everything off.

"I like tamari dressing too," I say to Alice.

"How old are you now, Benjy?" she asks.

"Eight."

"Aha!" She takes a sip of her wine. "That's just what I thought!"

"Really?"

"Uh-huh." Alice digs back into her salad again. "I was watching you before in the kitchen helping your mom set up. You're deep in industry versus inferiority."

I stare at the slick of tamari dressing soaking into my paper plate.

"I know," Alice goes on, chewing. "It sounds bad, right?"

"It kind of does," I admit.

"Psychosocial theory is funny that way." Alice squints closer at her salad and starts poking through it with a fork. "Where did that avocado go . . . I thought I had more avocado. Oh, well."

"Is it bad?" I finally ask.

"What?" Alice looks confused for a moment. "Oh, no, Benjy. God! There's no need for you to worry." She puts her hand softly on my arm. "Industry versus inferiority is really, really normative. It's the central crisis of the developmental stage you're in now." She gazes at me with a weird intensity. Her John Lennon glasses are smudged with grease. "You're dynamite."

Later, after we've put ourselves to bed and my mother and her friends are all sitting in a circle on the living-room floor to pass the pipe, the laughter and music in the other room keeps me awake. I lie in the dark with my eyes wide open, listening to the party through the bedroom door and trying to sift my mother's laugh from all the others. I know that I won't be able fall asleep until I pick out her laugh and hear it for myself, make sure that she's still there, that she's okay — but as soon as I find it, a high shriek followed by a sighing, swaying scale of hahahas, I would rather listen for her laugh again than fall asleep. After a while, I crawl out of bed and walk out to the front hallway in my PJs toward the music and the talking and the laughing, and I stand in the door-way looking in on the party until my mother notices me — until she sees me and sits straight up all of a sudden and says, "Oh, honey." The laughter falls a little softer; someone lunges at the stereo and turns down the Jackson Browne; my mother swoops over and takes me out into the hallway for a conference.

"What's wrong?" she asks. "Did you get frightened?"

"Everyone's laughing so much," I say to her. "I don't like all the laughing."

She kneels down and strokes the sides of my head. Her hands

feel hot. "I'll make sure we keep it down from now on," she says. "Promise. Will that make you feel better?"

"Yes," I say.

My mother is wearing one of her hand-embroidered shirts and a long skirt she's made by splitting a pair of jeans and sewing in an upside-down V of fabric on the back and the front. She can turn a pair of jeans into a skirt, my mother. I don't like it that she looks so nice either. Or the glossy look in her eyes.

"I feel awful that we kept you up," she says. "I'm sorry, Benjy. We'll be more quiet from now on, I promise."

"Why is everyone laughing so much?" I ask.

She sighs. "It's the weekend," she says. "We're smoking a little dope together and having fun. Dope makes grown-ups laugh. It helps us relax. You know the word 'groovy'?"

"Yes," I say.

"Well, we're feeling groovy."

"But what if something happens?" I ask.

"Nothing will happen," she says. "We're all safe."

"What if there's an emergency?"

"There won't be an emergency," she says. "I mean it."

"Will you stop laughing in time?"

"Of course I will," she says. "I'll be normal again. Just like that. If anything happens, I'll snap right out of it. You'll be safe."

"Will you?" I ask.

One Beehive in Nicaragua

IT'S NEW YEAR'S DAY, and I'm still broke. I started a ritual a few years ago at the urging of a psychic healer to wake up on New Year's Day and make two lists: on the first list are the things from the year before that I want to relegate to the dustbin, and on the second are my goals for the coming year, the things that I want to fulfill and to have in my life. Yes, I just wrote "psychic healer." What can I say? I was still in the backwash of the marital collapse, the economy had tanked, I had taken over a lease on the smallest one-bedroom I had ever seen in a part of Brooklyn I couldn't stand to be closer to Primo's preschool, and traditional therapy, as we have already seen, was not an option. So I thought I'd try something different — I saw my healer once, anyway — and I became, under her influence, the kind of magical thinker who makes lists to help align the planets in his favor and meditates every morning with his bare feet on the ground to hasten the outflow of negative energy. To be fair, none of what she taught me seems any crazier than hypnosis, or healing prayer, or believing the penis to be an object of widespread envy. In fact, it seems a little *less* crazy than what I've taken away from numerous attempts at reading Freud or the babble of strange tongues you are likely to hear on Sunday morning at your average suburban megachurch. What could be wrong with making a few lists to mark the end of the year and try to improve your life a little? Or performing a harmless spiritual exercise — barefoot — in the privacy of your own bedroom?

Laura, the psychic healer, saw her clients where she lived: in a little brick house tucked in a secret ivy-covered courtyard, complete with gardens and an apple tree, behind a row of old settlement houses in the West Village. It was a place that didn't seem possible, an enchanted island in the middle of the city. A gas fireplace burned in her kitchen. Everything in the house was precious, exotic, tiny. The floors leaned and the staircase to the second floor creaked with phantom steps. I had gone to see Laura with my friend Isabel, a journalist from Madrid who was the last person, next to me, who I would expect to tolerate an encounter with crystals and the spirit world. Isabel smoked too much, stayed out until daybreak with an ever-changing cast of expats from Europe and Latin America, read every important new novel that came out, and was rigorously skeptical of anything — in life, art, literature, fashion — that couldn't be verified. Plus, she had a wicked sense of humor. Going to see a healer had been her idea, and she was only doing it, I thought, on a lark. I needed help. I was still floundering. So I decided to follow Virgil's advice to Dante in *Inferno*: "*But you must journey down another road,*" he tells the lost poet, "*if ever you hope to leave this wilderness.*"

"*Querido* Ben," Isabel said on the phone the night before, "I'm getting a little worried about this psychic healing."

"Why?" I asked. "It's not a big deal. People see healers all the time. They're like a therapist plus massage. With a little therapy thrown in."

I heard Isabel take a drag on her cigarette. "They are?"

"Sure," I said. "They ask you a lot of questions, do an inventory of your past lives, wave a feather over you, and you're done. If you're lucky, you get a rubdown."

"Now you're joking with me," she said.

"Maybe," I admitted. "But it's not too far from what they do. You'll see."

"She wants us to arrive separately," Isabel said, pausing for another drag on her cigarette. "First me, then you. I'm the guinea pig. What if I disappear in a puff of smoke?"

"I'll go first if you want," I said.

"Oh, no," she said. "No freelancing. We do what the psychic healer says."

"You'll be fine. I promise."

"I hope so." She sighed. "*Querido* Ben, I really hope so."

I showed up at my appointed time, an hour later than Isabel was supposed to be there, and pressed the buzzer at a basement door on Jones Street. I waited. I peered into the window and saw a long corridor filled with bicycles and other junk. Nothing stirred. Isabel hadn't called or texted me about how her session had gone yet, and I hoped that I had come to the right place. When I pressed the buzzer again, I had one of those out-of-body experiences that come when you are doing something new, or nerve-racking, or a little dangerous. *I think I just pressed the buzzer where a psychic healer lives,* I told myself, *and I am waiting for her to let me in. I am standing here, on Jones Street, waiting for a psychic healer to let me in. It has come to this.* Laura arrived at the door breathless and ushered me through the long hallway and out to her secret courtyard, turning to chat with me along the way. She was small, bright, and wholesome-looking, like a women's studies major at a liberal arts school in the Midwest. She couldn't have been older than thirty-two. Her hair was pulled back in a scrunchie, and she wore leggings and a long cardigan—this was not the Stevie Nicks knockoff in vintage lace I'd been expecting. Laura apologized for the wait and explained, in the sunlight of her kitchen, that she was still finishing up her session with Isabel in the other room. She pointed me to the kitchen table and invited me to sit down. She handed me a pair of sound-canceling headphones for privacy. Then she was gone through the door and back to their session. I watched the gas flame pulsate in the fireplace. I couldn't hear anything in the next room, just the dull hiss of white noise. I took out my time-sucking Slab and punched out a few e-mails. When I looked up again, Laura had her arm around Isabel and she was leading her outside through the kitchen. Isabel was a wreck. I could tell that she'd been crying. Her eyes were red and puffy and her curls had gone wild. I took off my headphones and stood up.

"Are you all right?" I asked.

"I'm fine," Isabel said with a sniffle. "*Sí, sí.*"

"Are you sure?"

"Positive."

"Overlap is always uncomfortable," Laura said apologetically. She ferried Isabel out the door to the courtyard before I could ask her any more questions.* I watched them go with a feeling of dread. I wanted to get my life back. I wanted to feel better. Instead, there I was in a strange, spirit-filled kitchen, about to hand $90 that I could scarcely afford over to a psychic healer in a scrunchie who left her clients worse off than when they'd come in.

My fears about Laura were unjustified. Out of all the practitioners of the healing arts I've seen, whether I was dragged into their waiting rooms against my will or if I committed myself to

---

* Isabel has never told me what went wrong in her session with Laura. She doesn't like to talk about it. The most I've ever been able to get out of her, in a Japanese cocktail bar, was this: "Everything was going fine with the psychic healer, then all of a sudden I felt really shitty. I mean really shitty. You have no idea."

their discount furniture voluntarily, Laura was the most decent, the most selfless and honorable, and the only one who had a clue about how to help me. She started by asking me, quite simply, why I'd come to her. We were sitting across from each other in the living room, and the dread and nervousness I'd begun to feel earlier were already melting away. I gave Laura the same litany, more or less, that I had told to the therapist with the clementine in her front hallway: I was broke and in debt and tired of it, and I wanted to find a way to change my life. I spent most of my time either looking for work to cover my bills, or worrying about the fact that I could find enough, and if I did manage to find a job that paid well, like an assignment for a magazine, then the money quickly vanished thanks to all of my commitments, all of my outstanding bills. I had lost a career that I'd worked hard to build, at least it *felt* to me like "novelist" and "writer" were titles that I could no longer rightly claim, and I was still suffering the blowout from a marriage that hadn't simply ended in its first year, Hollywood style, as much as it had caught a spark and immolated. I had a son whom I loved more than anything else in life and I wanted to have more time with him. I wanted to fall in love again in the right way, with the right person, and I wanted to keep her and deserve her and take care of her and have a family. I wanted to write a book again instead of giving up halfway through and tossing another ambition on the funeral pyre. I wanted my life back. It was that simple. I wanted my life! I had mishandled it so badly when I was locked in dreams and didn't know any better that my life had left me too, found someone else to cook for and to sleep beside and to love with all of its might and to make happy. I stopped. I was not in tears. But I was not "all right." Laura was looking at me across the living room with a kindness that seemed infinite, then she told me, in two words, "You're grieving." I have no doubt that grief was written all over me. I shouldn't have needed a psychic healer to tell me this — but I did. She listened to me talking in her living room and made her diagnosis on the spot. I was stunned. I was embarrassed. It moved me. Oh, was I grieving. I could get out of bed in the morning and stand on two feet, I could walk upright, I could change Primo's Swaddlers and put him down for a nap and make him *pasta e ceci*; I could book travel online for articles I was writing and conduct interviews with experts on abstruse subjects I was trying to master and I could file my research neatly in folders and write draft after draft of a piece until my editors were happy; I could stand in front of a classroom filled with college students who were trying to become writers — some of them burned with it just like I had when I was sitting in their place, I could see it in their eyes and feel it emanating from them like heat — and pretend that I had its secrets figured out and I was in a position to teach them more than just the disappointments I had known at its hands, the mistakes, the uncertainties, the vanities it engorged, the grievances. I could do all of this. I could do it every day — and more. But then sometimes I would feel a wave of grief pass over me so strong, so concentrated in its power, that it sent me keeling forward. I would grab my knees and stay there, gasping for breath.

Oh, this was grief. Let me count the things I grieved. I was grieving for the morning I got married, when Marina had swooped into the house where we were having our wedding, late, and the mingling over coffee stopped. There she was: the woman I was marrying. I was grieving over the first, harried look we both shared in the hallway, Marina in her makeup and her dress, me in the Italian suit I've worn for the last time but I still can't throw away. I was grieving for the signal we gave our wedding guests to put down their coffee and their pastry plates where they were and start gathering in the music room; and for the way I waited for Marina to finish getting herself ready upstairs and then went after her and found her all alone in a spare bedroom, shivering with nervousness; and I grieved for the way it felt to throw my arms around her then, for the giddiness that came over us to be upstairs in our wedding clothes and alone like children with a roomful of guests waiting for us right below, waiting for us to come downstairs and have our wedding. I grieved for that. I grieved for all of it and more. I grieved for the rabbi's daughter, just six years old, who watched us exchanging our vows and said to her father afterward, "Wow, they really love each other." I grieved for that love and for having failed it. Did I ever fail it. We failed it well, at least. There is no going back. I grieved for the lesson that the rabbi's daughter learned that day: that love comes with no guarantees, no matter what the volume. I grieved for other loves too: for friendships I had lost, for the ambitions I had given up on out of impatience, weakness. I grieved for the books I had failed. For the career I might not have again. For the time I was missing with my son because he spent twenty days a month with my ex-wife and the Nominee, and I grieved for the love I'd begun to fear that I would never have again because I was broke and broken.

I don't know if Laura knew all of this about me. I have no idea what my "aura" told her about the sources of my grief. But I was draped in it. That much I do know. I was zipped up so tightly in my mourning parka that I could only lurch my way through life at half-speed, feel things through a layer of eiderdown padding. That's why, when Laura asked me to take off my shoes and socks and plant my bare feet on the floorboards, I did it. That's why I suspended my disbelief. I closed my eyes. Laura put her hands on me. I could feel them growing hot. I felt her taking hold of the things I grieved where I was storing them, one by one, and pull them out through the soles of my feet until they were no longer a part of me and I was free.

Here's how I began my "out with the old" list a year ago. I no longer have the original, given what I did with it, but a draft I just found in a notebook I was keeping at the time begins:

DEBT

BEING BROKE

SELF-DOUBT

MY DIVORCE

There are a few more items, in telling order:

ONLINE DATING

UNFINISHED PROJECTS

PROCRASTINATION

And then the last one, added almost as an afterthought:

TOO GOOD TO BE TRUE

This first list is meant to be burned to ash. You light a match, catch the list on a corner, and watch it go up in flames. It releases you from unhealthy attachments — or something like that. My apartment was so small on New Year's Day last year that I could light my list on fire at the stove, carry it across the living room, and toss it out on the fire escape before a single item had been burned. I yanked the window open. There was craggy snow on the rails outside and freezing air rushed in. I lit the front burner and caught the bottom corner of the list. It went up. Five steps and I had it out the window. Not everything burned the first time. I had to reach out on the fire escape and grab the remains. I still had DEBT, BEING BROKE, SELF-DOUBT, and MY DIV left over. I lit the list again and tossed it in the sink. That time it worked.

The second list is not for burning. I still have it. I kept it on my wall before I moved in with Eliza, right above the table I was using as my desk, and I used to read it through to start the day. It's not very long—just take the items on the burning list and turn them around:

TO PAY MY DEBTS
TO EARN ENOUGH TO LIVE
TO TRUST MYSELF
TO FINISH MY PROJECTS
TO KEEP MY WORD

I ended with the two things I wanted more than anything else. The life I wanted to have in broad strokes. I would have been embarrassed to write them on paper for most of my adult life—to admit that I had desires so obvious and needs so basic—but I was through pretending that I had it figured out. I had lost the privilege of my self-regard. I couldn't afford it anymore. The sin of pride had almost ruined me. I had been borrowing too heavily against the equity I had gained as a writer to prop up my floundering career. When I wrote TOO GOOD TO BE TRUE on the first list and burned it on the fire escape, I was trying to cast it all off. I was giving it away.

TO BE A GOOD FATHER

That I had no trouble writing. The desire to be a good father to Primo had welled up in me in the delivery room while he was still wriggling putty in a swaddling blanket and the better part amphibian. I had insisted beforehand that I would be there for his birth, and not the Nominee. He could sit it out. The baby was not his. Much to my surprise, Marina had agreed. It was better than the alternative I had imagined: working his arrival in shifts. We fought in the car all the way to the hospital once Marina's water broke, winding along the unmarked roads between her mother's house in Wellesley, Massachusetts, and the birthing center in Cambridge, where they'd been alerted we were on our way:

"How could you not print directions?" I wailed.

"I didn't think I needed to," she told me.

"You make a *route*. Everybody makes a *route*."

"They do?"

"Yes, they do!"

"Well, I didn't."

"You pack a bag! You make a route! You print directions!"

"My water just broke! Will you stop yelling at me?"

"Do you have any idea where we are?"

"Sort of . . ."

"This is *insane*!"

"Let me drive then!"

"No! That's even more insane!"

"Here, take this turnoff . . ."

"We're lost, Marina! We're lost because of *you*!"

Her labor was short and brutal, like something that happens at the back of a cave: she lay back on the birthing table with her knees up shouting, "Owww!" with every new contraction. I was on one side. Her friend R. was on the other, giving support and encouragement. Midwives and doctors rotated between Marina's legs until the time came. When he crowned, I saw a patch of skin and hair. It could have belonged to any animal. It didn't have to be a human being. One of the midwives gave us a voice-over narration. "He's crowning. Do you see the scalp? He has your hair color. In just a minute he'll be here and he'll say hello." I looked over at R. across Marina's knees and we shared an "Oh my fucking God" moment. When they pulled him out, Primo was a color I'd never seen before. Brown, with red smearing and purple undertones. He had been extruded from a tube and he looked it. They bundled him away to run their tests and take their measurements, and I couldn't keep my eyes off of him. He looked different from second to second—he was shape-shifting. Human clay. Once they'd snipped and clamped his cord and weighed him on a tray and swaddled him in blankets, they put him down under a heat lamp like a rack of prime rib and left him all alone. That's when I was hooked. Watching him on the table with a cap on and his mouth wide open, squirming into his body and trying to find his voice. *We made that,* I thought. *We made that in spite of everything.* I left Marina on the birthing table and went to stand near him. I hovered and staked my claim. He was mine. I was his. I could feel my loyalties undergo a seismic shift. I wanted to protect him. I trusted no one else to do it right. He needed me. I needed him. I looked back over my shoulder at the birthing table and they had Marina up in a crouch to push the afterbirth out into a tub of blood and amniotic fluid. I think the tub was a Rubbermaid.

I stood guard at the infant station until they picked him up and ferried him over to Marina for the big Nativity. Everybody gathered around to ooh and ahh. That hurt. It was the second part of my initiation into the fraternity of fathers: We are on a tier a little lower. We are a looming afterthought. We do not come first in a child's affections. I'm used to it. It's only natural, I guess. But still. The other night I was putting Primo to bed in the glow of his Ikea moon and he looked up at me from his pillow. I could tell that he had something on his mind—he had on his serious, talk-show interviewer face.

"You're small, Daddy," he said. I was sitting on the edge of the bed after our story time. Primo was wearing his winter PJs with blue stripes and rubberized feet, a gift from his *papou* and *yiayia*. He is already growing out of them. One more thing to add to the "to order when my next check comes" list—it is a long list.

"I'm not that small," I told him. He had taken me by surprise. I didn't expect to be defending my size at bedtime.

"Yes, you are." He seemed convinced. He rolled over and tucked his hands under his chin. "You're small."

"I haven't been going to the gym much," I admitted. "I should really do that more. I used to be bigger, you know."

"I want you to get smaller, Daddy."

"You do?"

He blinked with his long lashes. "Yup."

"How small do you have in mind?" I asked.

He thought about it for a second.

"I want you to be as small as me," he said.

The last item on the "good" list is the one I had the hardest time admitting. At least on paper. It seemed so personal. So *gooey*. Once I added it to the list, though, I felt relieved. I used to stare at it on the wall when I got hung up on my work, read it aloud to myself in a whisper over and over again. It was a prayer of sorts. Or maybe not of sorts: it was a prayer.

TO LOVE AND BE LOVED

I didn't write Eliza's name. I didn't need to. I was thinking about her when I wrote the list on New Year's Day last year and taped it to the wall. We'd already met at the reading on Court Street in Brooklyn, in an aisle between tables piled with new paperbacks. One of them was my first novel, which had been reissued a few months earlier. It felt good to have something I'd written back in bookstores. Eliza was with a friend she had dated for a little while; I was on a date with a writer who had just landed her own HBO series. (It was a setup gone wrong.) While my date drifted off to a corner to talk with another writer who already had an HBO series on the air, I started talking with Eliza. I noticed her profile first: I'll admit it. She is like someone out of time. I was more surprised to find her at a bookstore with a red Gore-Tex rain jacket under one arm than I would have been to stumble on her in a museum, poised on a pedestal with great feathered wings and holding out a victory garland. All right, the goddess Nike might not have been the first thing that came to mind that night. I have let the way I feel about Eliza influence my description. But after we talked in the bookstore and I was leaving with my date to complete the awkward ritual of our first dinner at a faux bistro down the block (even more awkward: she paid), I felt something tugging me back to Eliza. I turned around to look over my shoulder and tried to catch another glimpse. I knew right away that she was someone to win. Someone to deserve. I had no way of seeing the future when I turned to look for her through the bookstore window. I didn't know that she would feel the same and find me online a few days later. From there we took our time. A dinner at a restaurant in her neighborhood that I remember for the way she sat with her back to the windows and the darkness of a winter night in Fort Greene falling still behind her. A few weeks later I made her dinner in my miserable apartment. She was sweet about it. "I guess it is a little small," she said on her way back from the twenty-second tour. That was right before Christmas. Eliza was on her way to the Adirondacks to spend the holiday with her family, and I was taking Primo to Massa-chusetts for our annual tour to see both sets of grandparents. We exchanged flirty e-mails during our separate travels — not too desperate or too many, which I found encouraging. I missed her already. It was nice to miss someone.

She wrote me on the twenty-ninth:

hope you guys are having fun in Gloucester (?). it's been snow-ing like crazy here! our driveway is so slippery we haven't been able to drive anywhere for two days. kind of fun, though — only travelling by skis & snowshoes. tonight we go to lake placid to see scott hamilton attempt to re-create his famous back-flip on ice.

I wrote back:

Sounds like the perfect Christmas to me, Eliza. We've had a great time too. Primo didn't want to leave. At a rest stop on the highway now, but I'll write later when I have the chance.

I hope Scott Hamilton doesn't break a hip!

Typos courtesy of iPhone

Then I wrote again, from home in Brooklyn:

Well, by now Scott Hamilton should be flying through the air at the Olympic skating rink in Lake Placid and your niece and nephew are either excited, bored or scarred for life. (Seriously: I hope they have an ambulance waiting in the wings like they do at hockey games. That guy must be 55.) The trip back from Gloucester — your spelling was impeccable — was uneventful, if a little long. For a while I thought I might have to resort to stopping at the Swedish warehouse in New Haven for some run-around time and a bowl of mac and cheese for 99 cents, but by then Primo was napping and I managed to make it to Bridgeport before he woke up. I'm taking just a few minutes while he's in the bath to write you, so I'll probably have to sign off soon.

And later still, I got Eliza's report from Lake Placid:

He made it! Unbelievable. The entire stadium was on its feet cheering. Though when you realize he's only 4 feet tall, it makes the feat somewhat less impressive, as he really doesn't have to get that far off the ground.

Anyway, the whole thing was just the sort of grand cheese festival you'd expect, complete with Journey & Genesis songs and red leather pants and sequined halter tops. Somehow the whole town of Lake Placid seems to be permanently trapped in the amber of 1984 . . . which is kind of perfect once you've had two margaritas at dinner, like I and the rest of the grown-ups did.

This year we packed Primo in the car and made a stop in Massachusetts to see my mother and her partner, Jan — his grandma and *méme* — before we continued on to the Adirondacks for Christmas Eve. Primo was excited for the trip. With his grannies, he got to be helper when my mother made her Swedish cookies and load the woodpile with the little red wheelbarrow his *méme* found for him, while with Eliza's family he had a sledding hill to look forward to with a view of the High Peaks. We had brought him with us to the Adirondacks a few times before and he knew the rituals: filling backpacks with sandwiches and water bottles for family hikes through moss-dripping woods, leaving room for cookies that we broke out on the mountain peaks, sprawled lazy and exhausted on the ledges from the climb; waking to a fire in the hearth and the crackling of the logs; opening the gate to the Lake Road with a secret knock for the gnomes that only he and Eliza knew; finding a shelf mushroom for every visit and taking it home to draw a picture on the spongy underside and hang it with all the others in the living room; filling the bird feeders on the porch and waiting for the nuthatches to come back and the chipmunks to scurry underneath on the deck in search of seeds; turning the lofts above the bedrooms into clubhouses with Eliza's niece and nephew and dreaming up games with ever-changing rules, yelling down for a grown-up when they needed a referee. After our first weekend with Eliza and her family, Primo announced to me, "Daddy, I *always* want to go to the Adirondacks." I didn't tell him about the time a bear had broken in through a screen door when Eliza was alone in the house one summer and spent a long, debauched night in the pantry while she was barricaded in her bedroom clutching an empty Heineken bottle in one hand and a heavy iron statue of Hanuman, the Hindu monkey god, in the other.

Primo gasped when he saw the Christmas tree. It wasn't technically a tree — it was a treetop. The highest reaches of a sixty-foot Douglas fir that a forester had saved for Eliza's parents and felled for them before the holidays. We had just come in with our snow-dusted bags to hugs and greetings in the entryway. Boots of all sizes lined the wall in neat pairs and a table by the door was strewn with fur-lined hats and ski gloves. Eliza's mother, Margot, had gone straight to Primo and asked, "Can you help me light the Christmas tree?" He nodded and said a quiet, "Yeah." I'd been prepared for what to expect from Christmas in the Adirondacks with Eliza's family. I believe her exact words to me had been: "You mean Christmas village? It's ridiculous." She had meant it fondly. We followed Margot and Primo into the living room and

I saw the tree: it stretched high into the beams of their log camp. The treetop's boughs were spare and winding, as if they'd been sculpted by the mountain winds. Even bolted into its stand, the tree looked like something wild and unreachable. The province of eagles and great horned owls. Eliza's mother had draped the boughs with lights and gold and silver balls and strings of red wooden beads that looked like necklaces. A train track circled the base of the tree and there was an electric locomotive waiting front and center, right where the presents would go once the children fell asleep.

"Primo!" Eliza's niece called from the TV room downstairs. "Do you want to watch a movie with us? I promise it's not scary . . ."

"He's lighting the tree now, darling," Margot called downstairs. "Just give us a minute."

"All right!" she yelled back. "But hurry up! This is the best part!"

"It's not the best part!" her seven-year-old brother hollered from the TV room. "This part is boring!"

"Don't listen to him!"

Primo turned on the power strip with Margot's help and the tree flashed on with a Milky Way of pinpoint lights. We took a moment to stand there and admire it. The fire licked a pyramid of logs in the hearth. Jack, a high-strung standard poodle, dozed in a big pile of pillows on the couch. The High Peaks surrounded their camp in a snowcapped bowl. You could see new snow squalls dusting the mountains' shoulders far in the distance.

"It's so beautiful," Eliza said in gratitude. "It's astonishing. Look at that tree!"

"It's one of your best," Eliza's stepfather said at the hearth. Wade had just come out of the shower and he had slicked his hair back with a comb. He was in his Christmas plaid and had a sweater tied around his neck. "A real beauty. That fir must have been a giant."

"What do you think?" Margot said to Primo. "Is that your kind of Christmas tree? Do you think Santa's going to like it?"

"Uh-huh," he said.

"I just love it," Eliza said, turning to beam at me. "Didn't I tell you?"

"You did," I said. "It's incredible. I'm not sure I believe it."

$191.63. I had that number stuck in my head all through Christmas. It was my Five Golden Rings, my Eleven Pipers Piping. That's how much I've been bringing home every week in unemployment, and it's my only steady income until I start to teach again next semester. Then I'll be getting a raise to $600 every two weeks, the going rate for adjuncts in the Ivy League. At least I'll be earning it; that's what I told myself every morning when I woke up early to a sleeping house and went out to put on the first pot of coffee. It wasn't much, but I could build from it. I had to start with a net positive instead of something else I had borrowed or bought on credit. I had to start. Christmas Village had its wonders, and I enjoyed them all: Bundling up after a big breakfast to head to the sledding hill in a cold so clear and crystalline it bloomed our cheeks red and I could feel it burning in my lungs with every breath. It was how winter used to be in childhood. Pulling an inner tube filled with two squealing kids across the snowy fields by a rope and sinking into the snowdrifts up to my knees. "I want faster!" Primo ordered while I dragged them ahead. The wind was blowing the freshest snow up in swirls. "Go faster, Daddy! Go faster!" Pushing Primo and Eliza down the hill together on the quickest sled and watching them fly over bumps and hit the deepest snowdrift at the end of the run and roll off with twin shrieks. Climbing Owl's Head one day with adults, kids, and dogs and sitting bundled on the peak for a rest while clumps of snow drifted down like little parachutes. Carrying Primo down the mountain on my shoulders and ducking every time he grabbed a snow-covered tree branch and dusted us in a cloud of ice crystals. "It's snowing, Daddy!" $191.63. It was an amount that wouldn't leave me alone. I tried not to dwell on it, but it was hard. I was there on a scholarship from the Fresh Air Fund. I was the only welfare case in Christmas Village. I was turning forty-two. I loved my son. I loved Eliza.

On Christmas Eve, after we'd had our stone crab claws flown in from Florida and Primo had squealed his way through a bubble bath in the Jacuzzi, I went out to the Christmas tree with my envelope. It was the only present that I'd brought with us. Downstairs, the Ping-Pong table had been turned into a present-wrapping operation. There were loads coming upstairs, and presents being divvied up, and ribbons being tied. I didn't know where they would fit them all. The electric train had already been buried in an avalanche of presents. Primo had his share coming; he'd already opened a haul of presents from his grandparents. I found a hollow in the boughs and tucked my envelope in with the lights and the ornaments. It fell out and landed on the presents. I picked it up and found a better place to leave it on the treetop. It was a white envelope. Primo had written "Eliza" on the front in blue marker. Inside there was a card stating that a beehive would be given to a family in need in Nicaragua in her name. Thirty dollars. That's what it had cost — that's all I could afford. Primo had picked the beehive out from the choices in the charity's catalog. It was his present to Eliza. I knew she would be happy with it. There were no other presents under the tree from me. None for her; none for Primo; none for anyone in Eliza's family. Eliza had signed my name to all the presents we had brought from the city, but she had picked them out and paid for them herself. She had even paid for the presents we had given my family. That envelope was it: my Christmas. One beehive in Nicaragua.

Later, while I was lying in bed next to Eliza, I couldn't sleep. She was still up with a book. I stared at the ceiling. I rolled over. I threw the covers off and sat up.

"There's something wrong," I said.

She looked up from her book in a sudden panic. "Did you hear something? Was there a noise?"

"No," I said. "I mean with me."

Eliza searched my face for what seemed like a long time. Then she put aside her book and turned to me. The light from the birchbark reading lamp next to her was warm and veined with shadows. "Tell me," she said. "Tell me what it is."

"I can't talk about it."

"Why not?" she asked.

"It's too much," I said. "It's Christmas Eve."

"Tell me," she pleaded.

"I'll try," I said. "But I can't do it now."

She lay her head on my chest. "It's okay. I'm right here."

"I can't do it yet."

"Shh," she said. "I'm here."

At the Wheel of the Haunted Sedan

IT'S TIME TO TELL the story of how I lost my ex-wife to the Nominee. His nickname is a relic of the night he laid the major groundwork. I was not there. I was tossing and turning in a strange bedroom—just one of many sleepless nights to come that year; I will never take for granted a good eight hours again, waking from deep oblivion and knowing nothing but the light, the fact of being conscious, the clutch of my own hand down my underwear—in a sunny, multilevel house I was renting on a duck pond in Maryland, while Marina threw herself into after-partying back in New York City. It was the night of a Major Literary Awards dinner. Black tie, red wine from Slovenia, tributes to Oprah, a high-wattage emcee. The Nominee's loss in the fiction category that year was only cover for his hunger to steal something. That's right: I guess he worked the noble-loser angle on my wife. I had thought that one belonged to me. But let me back up. This is going too fast and I want to get it right. I'll start with the geese. Or, as I muttered while I heard them flying all-nighters overhead on their journey south, cleaning out their windpipes with a sound that still makes me shudder every time I hear it,

HOWANK-HOWANK-HOWANK-HOWANK-HOWANK-HOWANK, "fucking geese."

Or when they took off in great clouds at dawn, honking their intentions idiotically, or stood mutely by the hundreds in muddy fields, shitting on their feet and daring anyone to shoot them. Geese. I had never seen as many geese as I did that fall and winter on the Eastern Shore. Marina was supposed to be with me while I spent the year teaching at a sleepy middle-tier school on a river, an experiment to see how we could handle another kind of life—but she was not. We had planned on trying to get pregnant while we were out of the city, but as of the night she chose the Nominee, or he chose her, she had slept in the house I'd rented for us twice. The geese. It was me and the megalopolis of geese in transit. They were an angry mob in the sky, fleeing for sunsets on the beach and easier living. That neat V-formation flying didn't fool me for a minute. They were dumb. They were spiteful. They were loud. They were reckless. They were mean to other geese. The sky was sloppy with them. There were too many geese loose in the world. HOWANK-HOWANK-HOWANK-HOWANK-HOWANK-HOWANK. Fucking geese.

I'd had a bad feeling, I admit, from the day I arrived on campus. By myself, in a Volvo station wagon that would be my second home—or maybe it was my first, in hours logged—all that year. It was August, and the days were sweltering. I'd driven through wastelands of industrial New Jersey, strips of malls and auto dealerships in Delaware, fields in Maryland that sprouted instant housing developments with gates and wood rail fences before turning back into sunbaked fields. The college where I was going to be teaching had a gate of its own, an academic quad, dorms and houses and stately brick administration buildings; there was a library and a gym and even a boathouse on the riverfront downtown, a quaint tidy village with antique shops and

B&Bs and narrow backstreets where the houses were all built in the Federal style — a destination for weekenders and retirees from bigger cities who wanted to buy the paper every day in the same overstuffed curio shop and sip twenty-ounce lattes in the shade of tree-lined sidewalks where no one was in a hurry. There was a waterfront with a walkway for strolling, redbrick mansions built by riverboat captains and merchants from a more bustling past, a theater, and a restored hotel with balconies. It shouldn't have felt like I was arriving to serve out a sentence. I shouldn't have had to pull over inside the campus gate, the engine still running and the air conditioner blowing fog, and press my forehead against the steering wheel.

"This is not a disaster," I said aloud. "I will be all right. This is not going to be a disaster."

I called Marina.

"That was quick," she said. I had caught Marina rushing to a yoga class — she was always on her way to yoga, or coming back from yoga, or unavailable while she was doing yoga in Manhattan. After years of being a star student on the mat, Marina had spent the summer getting her certification to teach. It was a mystery to me, all the time and energy she devoted to her yoga practice in the company of strangers, in sweltering rooms that smelled of feet, but I was trying to be supportive. I was trying to be a good husband. I had strayed first, so my job was to be superhumanly perfect. She has been wronged, which earned her the right to run roughshod over me while she worked out her feelings on the yoga mat. Or didn't.

"Where are you?" I asked.

"There's a two thirty with Lily at the Shala," she gasped at full speed. I could hear the traffic behind her and she was out of breath. "If I can make it."

"Lily."

"You know, *Lily.*"

"Oh, right."

There was a loud interruption while something happened to the phone — she had probably just lost her hold on it, but it sounded like Marina had entered a tear in the universe between the F train and the yoga studio. She came back. (Or did she? Did she ever come back?)

"What time is it now?" she asked in a panic.

I lifted my head from the steering wheel to check the clock on the dashboard. "Two forty."

"Shit." I heard her picking up the pace. "I'm always late for Lily's class. Why am I always late for Lily?"

Why are you always late, I thought. *Lily doesn't know waiting. Lily gets paid the same no matter when you show up for her 2:30. She's a yoga teacher with tattoos who carries a guitar case everywhere, probably empty, and sprinkles rose petals over her students while they're meditating. Lily doesn't even know that she's waiting for you to show up. Lily can wait.*

"How far are you?" I asked.

"On Broadway! I can see it!"

"You'll make it." I sighed. "It's a little weird here. I'm not sure about it yet." I looked out at the campus, which was suspiciously empty for a school about to start its fall semester. A delivery truck was parked ahead with its cargo bay wide open, at the rear of a big building with a spire on its peak that must have been important, but no one seemed to be loading or unloading it. "I might have done the wrong thing."

"Can we talk about it later?" Marina asked.

"Sure."

"Call me . . ."

"Have a good yoga," I said, but she had already hung up. I could see her in a controlled sprint down the crowded sidewalks of lower Broadway, weaving through the clots of people with her hair tied up and her favorite tie-dyed minidress on over her tank top and yoga pants. When we first started dating, I used to wait for her on the street outside her favorite yoga studio on Lafayette and watch the doors for her, feeling a throb of disappointment every time a new lithe, impossible beauty pushed through the doors to the street, still flushed from the mysterious exertions she had undergone in the Temple upstairs, and it wasn't Marina. I kept on waiting. It didn't really matter how long; I just waited on the street with the other boyfriends, feeling lucky that Marina was mine. New York—and our life together—felt very far away all of a sudden, farther away in hours, miles, and geography than I had gone since I left that morning, alone in the car with my duffel bags and boxes of books; so did Marina.

So did Marina.

Once, when I was twelve or thirteen, I woke up early on a weekend—I don't know if it was a Saturday or a Sunday, the only difference in my family was what I'd watch on TV—with a very distinct feeling, a premonition so clear that it was almost a command: that I should get up out of bed, go over to my window, and look down at the street. I did. In my T-shirt and boxer shorts, the nightly uniform I'd graduated to from PJs. The house was still quiet when I got up; not even our dog, Dusty, a grumpy terrier mix, was making any noise. We had moved to our neighborhood, in a suburb west of Boston, just the year before, and I was still getting used to everything about it: the neatly trimmed hedges, the lawns and driveways, the hoodies all the kids in my class wore and the crappy music they listened to (Billy Squier, Iron Maiden). My mother had bought the house with her partner, Jan, in a surge of hopeful excitement and they would be living together openly as a lesbian couple, at least as openly as they could be about it in 1982. Our street was one of the larger traffic arteries, so it was wide and lined on both sides by trees. Some of the trees were so old and tall that the roots broke through the sidewalks in places, heaving the bricks and concrete slabs up at odd angles. I pulled the curtains back and looked out from the second-story window: nothing. I heard birds. It was a peaceful morning in the suburbs. While I stood there looking out, I saw a car appear at the top of the hill and start to glide down in my direction. It was a green sedan, an older American car with a black hardtop — a Buick or a Dodge — and I could hear the puttering of its engine as it got farther down the hill and closer to our house. That's when the strange thing happened: the reason I remember waking up that morning, the premonition whispered in my ear, the silver-green color of the old sedan. While I watched, the car made a slow, gliding swerve from the center of the street toward the sidewalk and one of the older trees. It felt like déjà vu, something I'd seen in a movie or in a dream. I thought, *That car is about to hit a tree.* And that's what I saw from my bedroom window, what I saw unfolding from the second floor, in a kind of slow motion, without being able to stop it or tell anybody about what I was seeing: the car floated toward the massive tree, rode up onto the curb, glanced its nose off the trunk, and, for a moment, hung there sideways in the air before flipping onto its roof and landing with a sickening crunch. It all happened slowly — achingly slow — outside my window as I watched. I thought about yelling. I thought about running downstairs in my boxers and opening the front door. But the same voice in my head said to me, *Don't move. Watch what happens next.*

First, there was the dog. A black standard poodle. I remember its curls. The dog crawled out of the car, I think it was in the backseat, and took off running up the hill toward home, whining and yelping. The driver, a woman, crawled out of the car next, on her hands and knees, and she got to her feet unsteadily to watch the poodle galloping away. She lifted her hands to her face and called its name. (I can no longer recall the poodle's name — Ginger? Oscar? Freddy?) The dog was still yelping in the distance, the sound growing smaller and thinner and shriller. She turned to look at the car, still lying on its roof in the middle of the street, and then she looked down at her body as if to scan for injuries. No one came running out of their houses to see what the commotion was. It was too early for traffic. The birds, after a brief respite, were singing again. I didn't dare move from my place at the window. I could hardly breathe. The woman stood by the car for another long moment, clearly coming to a decision about what to do next, then she crossed her arms and started after the dog on foot. I watched her walk up the hill, stopping to call out the dog's name throughout the neighborhood, until she crossed into the trees and I couldn't see her anymore. The wreck was cleared away on a flatbed by midmorning, while I watched TV, and for a long time after that, I would get an eerie feeling every time I looked across the street and saw the deep gouge in the tree from the car's impact, a shiver that used to make my scalp tingle and my sphincter clinch.

I never understood why the premonition woke me up that morning and sent me to the bedroom window, or what happened inside the car that made the woman lose control and head straight for the tree. Now I think there was some design in it all. I do not know the author, if there was one. I do not know why I was chosen that morning to get up out of bed and be a stranger's witness. Here's one idea: when the semester got under way on the Eastern Shore and I had a sinking feeling that my life was heading for a calamity that I could neither avoid nor see; when my days started with a low-grade dread that I tried to talk myself out of or chase away by picking up the phone and calling Marina back home in Brooklyn, and this dread built gradually over the course of every day until I knew it — yes, I knew — with a fair degree of certainty that I was at the wheel of the haunted sedan this time and the appointment with the tree was mine; when I had tried everything I knew to avoid a reckoning and still the tree kept on growing larger in the windshield, then at least I would know, thanks to what I saw that morning, that I could survive, and I also knew there was the chance, and maybe even a good one, that someone else would wake from sleep and come to their window, early in the morning, to watch over me. I would have a witness too. It would not just be me, a long, slow glide into a car crash, and the crazed HOWANK-ing of the geese.

I had a routine all that fall that I stuck to in a dogged search for regularity: I woke up on the early side, somewhere in the sevens, made a pot of coffee and a bowl of oatmeal in the kitchen, then I brought my laptop out on the screened-in porch and "wrote" for the next two hours. I have put "wrote" in quotation marks because I didn't actually manage to do much writing — instead, I rewrote everything I had started on the computer screen over and over until the spark of life had been extinguished and the paragraphs had a perfect, sculptural look. No uneven line breaks; no stacks of "the" or "and"; no repeated words. It is a kind of obsessive polishing made possible only by the computer, and it burns the hours just like real work does, but in fact it is the opposite: a fail-safe system for killing off writing with maximum effort. Once I had toggled the piece I was working on to death, I would file it in away in FALSE STARTS and open up a new file in Word to begin the process all over again. At ten or so, with the woods around me echoing with the cracking of branches, the chirruping of songbirds, and the rustling of chipmunks in the fallen leaves, the porch would begin to tremble and I would hear the far-off rumble of explosions. Ordnance, the professor I was renting from explained to me, at the military's Aberdeen Proving Grounds on the other side of the Chesapeake. The bombs and artillery fire were my signal to shower and start getting ready for my trip to campus — sometimes the concussions followed me to the bathroom, shaking the medicine cabinet while I shaved, thumping in the distance as I chose the day's professor outfit from the closet, vibrating the clock radio on the bedside table while I sat on the unmade bed and left another voice mail for Marina:

"Hey, it's me. You must be at yoga. I'm heading to campus now and I thought I'd try and catch you . . . It's lonely here. I didn't sleep much last night. Give me a call later, okay?"

I dealt with the daily in-swell of e-mails in my office: Students making excuses for why they weren't coming to class, which started out plausible at the beginning of the semester ("i woke up feeling, really really bad professor. i am taking the day off from classes so i wont puke") but grew gradually more baroque as time went on ("sorry professor but i had an allergic reaction i think to shellfish," "today I have to be fitted for splints to alleviate my Carpal Tunnel," "there was a bad robbery at my dorm," etc.). Department e-mails I was copied on that came in floods and might as well have been the work of spam-generating mills in India instead of professors on the other side of campus. Invitations to upcoming lectures and public events, some of which I helped organize, that came nowhere near to filling the lecture halls and function rooms where they were held, and usually ended with a catered reception for the campus guest and the Serial Attenders, the same core group of faculty and administration officers who came to everything and huddled, afterward, around the orb of warm artichoke dip, heated by a can of Sterno, that Dining Services had made famous. I did my best to pay attention at the events that I went to, trying to hide my loneliness behind a mask of feigned interest, the same expression that I'd worn through college and grad school, then I grabbed a plate with the others and I joined the line around the orb, waiting for an opening.

"Tried the dip?" a professor from my department would ask while forking in a plateful.

"Oh, yes," I said. "I've been initiated."

"It should be criminal, this dip," another Serial Attender chimed in.

"You mean it isn't?"

"Not in the state of Maryland!"

"Well, if it is," the first professor said, wheeling around to join the line again, "I'm a recidivist."

Laughter around the orb. More dip.

"How's your wife?" I got that one a lot. Marina had come down for my second interview and had met some members of the faculty over lunch. *You're Jewish!* one professor had gushed at first sight, practically reaching out and cupping Marina's face in her hands. *We need more Jewish noses here! More interesting faces!* That might, I realized, have been the moment when Marina had decided, at least in her heart, not to join me on the Eastern Shore. I thought that was unfair of her. The professor's enthusiasm had been genuine. We had our plan, and I was sticking to it.

"She's fine," I said. "Too busy. It's hard to peel her away from the city."

"Is she in Brooklyn?"

"Yes."

"We haven't seen her."

"*So* lovely."

The serving spoon was passed to me. I took it gratefully and started digging into the greasy round of dip. The silver orb was emptying quickly.

"She'll come down soon," I said. "Right now I'm driving back on weekends."

"Oh, really?"

"That's a trip."

"Quite boring, I find."

"It's all right," I claimed. "I have my Wawa and Starbucks stops mapped out. I'm a big fan of the Vince Lombardi rest area."

"Are you done with the spoon?" another Serial Attender asked, eyeing my portion greedily. "I haven't had my crack at the dip."

The house I had rented for us was tucked into a pine wood that fringed a pond and the surrounding fields. It had a long dirt driveway ending at a woodpile, picture windows that made it feel like a tree house, decks on every floor with a view of the pond, a big sunken living room with a fireplace. A dishwasher and garbage disposal in the kitchen, a washer and a dryer in the basement—all the creature comforts that seem like unimaginable luxuries when you're used to apartment living in New York. It was cheap too, at least by Brooklyn standards. We had originally planned on subletting our place in Carroll Gardens for the year and saving money. But Marina's mother was facing another round of chemotherapy, in Boston, and Marina wanted to be closer than she would have been in Maryland—or so she said. We kept both places. It stretched our finances, but the rental on the pond was only for the fall, and I could find a smaller and cheaper place in the spring, even just a room in town, if Marina ended up staying behind for the whole academic year. It was just a season, I told myself in the supermarket, buying iceberg lettuce that I would slice in half and eat with a can of tuna fish at the kitchen counter, not even bothering to sit. I was living through a season of life, and it would turn.

When I got home from campus every afternoon, sometimes

later if there was an event or if I had stopped in my office to meet with students or correct their papers, I would wander the house from room to room with a cordless phone, talking to my absent wife.

"They've been asking about you," I would say.

"Who is?" she asked.

"The faculty." I was standing in the room that she'd picked as her office when we agreed to rent the house. It was a cozy, book-lined study off the master bedroom on the second floor. There was a desk with a view of the pond, a daybed for napping and lying down to read, a small balcony with a sliding screen door. I hardly set foot in the room unless I was on the phone with Marina. "You've got a following."

"There?" she scoffed. "In Chesterville?"

"Chestertown," I corrected her.

"Chesterfield, whatever."

"It's Chestertown."

I could hear her banging around pots and pans in the kitchen. She was in one of her angry, teenage moods. They happened more often now that she was spending all of her time on yoga, which seemed a little strange to me. But what did I know? It just made me miss the Marina I had married more, because she hadn't been like this. She had been flaky, and late, and unreliable, and full of theories about the way the world worked that didn't make any sense, but she hadn't been angry all the time. This was new. It had started when she stood underneath the chuppah with me, in our wedding clothes, and said, "I do."

"I'm not coming down," she insisted, turning on the water at the sink, "to be a good little faculty wife. I can't even believe you *took* that job."

"That's not what you said before," I reminder her. "You used to think it was a great idea. We both did."

"Well, I changed my mind," she said.

"I get that."

"I'm allowed to, you know."

"That's true," I told her. "And I'm allowed to feel shitty about it."

Marina shut off the water. "You'll live."

I slid the screen door open and stepped out on the balcony. The geese were starting to arrive at the pond, in smaller waves at first, settling down into the green water and feeding in the muck before they took off again on their journey. It would get worse — much worse — later in the fall, when the true hordes arrived. Already, I could hear their HOWANK-ing echo over the phone line.

"We had a plan," I reminded her again. "I made a commitment when I took the job. I'm not backing out of it."

"I'm so glad," she said, and slammed another pot.

"You're glad what?"

"That you're *honoring* your *commitments*," she said witheringly.

"Are you serious?"

"Yes, I'm serious."

"Marina, this has to stop."

"I know," she said more quietly.

"I mean it."

HOWANK-HOWANK-HOWANK-HOWANK.

"What's that noise?" Marina asked.

I sighed. "Geese. They're migrating."

"To your house?"

"It only sounds like it."

"They're so loud. What a racket."

Another wave was arriving, staking out the water before settling down with a collective splash.

"I know." I took a deep breath. "The pond is like an airport. I can hear them all night."

"Well," she went on, slamming another pot, "I'm not coming to Chesterville. You can tell the faculty *that*. Me and my funny Jewish nose are staying right here."

"So where does that leave me?" I asked.

"I don't know."

"You don't know," I echoed.

HOWANK-HOWANK-HOWANK-HOWANK.

SPLASHHHHHHHHH.

"Are you coming this weekend?" she asked.

"I think so."

"Good," she said. "You can come to my Saturday morning class."

"Yoga?"

"What else would it be?" she asked.

"I'm not sure I'm ready for you to be my yoga teacher," I told her.

"Why not?"

I looked out at the trees, the back patio, and the planters I'd been watering with a garden hose twice a week when it didn't rain.

"I want you to be my wife."

HOWANK-HOWANK-HOWANK-HOWANK . . .

There was a dock at the edge of the pond on the property, rotting and falling apart from neglect, and a canoe with broken gunwales, a missing paddle, and three inches of stagnant water pulled up on the shore. I had an invitation to use the boat for fishing, but I wasn't really tempted. I'd been more interested when I rented the house in a pair of green deck chairs set under a tree at the end of the winding path through the woods to the pond. They had a nice view of the water; I had imagined sitting there with Marina at the end of my teaching day with a book and a glass of wine. I had never really fantasized or even thought that much about what married life with her would be like, how it would be different from the years we had already spent as a couple — so far it was just like it had always been before we decided to get married, only worse. There was more distance between us, more that went unsaid, more that left both of us feeling dissatisfied, hurt, or angry. At first I ignored the chairs down at the water. If I saw them through the window when I looked out toward the pond, or caught a glimpse of them, between the trees, while I came down the driveway in the Volvo at end of the day — two rickety green chairs, sitting side by side — I felt a pang in my heart that I hated, but it was real. I didn't like missing my wife the way I did, and it bothered me that when I daydreamed about sitting with her at the pond it was like something from a commercial for instant coffee, and it bothered me even more that I had to daydream about Marina sitting next to me in our rickety green chairs at the pond instead of being able to pour a drink, pick up a book, and meet her there after another day of dealing with campus weirdness.

    —*It's so peaceful here,* Marina said to me in the daydream.

    —*I know. It is.*

I settle in and sip my drink.

    —*Remember when you didn't want to come? I ask.*

    —*I do.*

    —*And?*

    —*I still hate Chesterville.*

    —*It's Chestertown.*

We gaze out over the water. I open up my book.

    —*But I'm glad I'm here.*

One night, after I tried to find Marina on her cell phone and the call had gone straight to voice mail, and listening to NPR in the kitchen while I chopped my nightly head of iceberg wasn't enough to distract me from the fear that I was losing her, I poured myself a whiskey — a deep one, with lots of ice — and headed out to the pond to watch the geese from "our" chairs. It was dusk, and the nights were starting to get chilly. I heard the ice rattling in my tumbler as I followed the path through the woods.

The air traffic at the pond had been picking up as of late; sometimes the geese were so thick in the fields when I drove home from campus that I felt a sudden urge to turn my wheel and plow off-road to make them scatter; at other times the fields were empty save a handful of white snow geese or an angry pair of mallards, looking lost or as if the others had forgotten them. Maybe I should have felt a greater sense of wonder about the geese in all their plenitude. It was the first time I had ever felt an allegiance with the hunter and not the animals they hunted: you could have shot the geese all day long, I thought, and ringed your duck blind with spotlights and fired indiscriminately into the skies until dawn, and *still* they would have kept on coming in waves. There was a terrible surplus of geese in the world, and they were taunting me with their righteousness, their stupid goose telepathy.

Back to the chairs by the pond: I chose the chair that looked like it had been splattered with the least amount of goose shit, wiped it down with a handful of leaves, and settled in with my whiskey. I heard the rapid-fire knocking of a woodpecker, high in the trees. The geese were quiet for the moment, floating in their tight formations and clucking. Diving and popping right back up. They took no note of me. I sipped my whiskey. I looked over at the empty chair beside me, spattered with fresh turds. This was not my vision of married life; it was nothing like my daydream. Marina was not sitting next to me in her yoga pants and bare feet, her posture so eerily perfect in her chair that she looked like she was levitating while she pored through her copy of *Yoga Mala* by Sri K. Pattabhi Jois. I could not ask her, finally, *Can you explain why yoga is so important all of a sudden? Why your mother is having chemotherapy up in Boston and I rented a house for us in Maryland and you are almost exactly in between, doing yoga? Can you explain that to me? Can you tell me why this is happening?* I could not get an answer; she could not get any of the answers to her own questions, the things she was waiting to find out from me. The things that woke up with us in Brooklyn, and followed us through our days there, running the usual week-end errands and seeing people, and hung between us like fog on a mirror that we were too afraid to clear. I sat there for a long time, lost in thought, letting the geese ignore me while I sipped my drink. Then I shut my eyes and listened to the rippling of the pond and the restless paddling of the birds until I gave in to my tiredness and drifted asleep.

When I woke up again, I'm not sure how much later, the next wave of geese had arrived and the sky above the pond was dark with their neat diving bodies and their flashing wings as they settled down into the water in sortie after sortie.

HOWANK-HOWANK-HOWANK-HOWANK . . .

WHY ARE YOU ALONE? they taunted me.

THE OTHER CHAIR, they said. IT'S EMPTY.

WHAT HAPPENED TO YOUR WIFE?

HOWANK-HOWANK-HOWANK-HOWANK . . .

WHAT HAPPENED TO YOUR WIFE?

WHERE IS SHE?

Not This Guy

DEAR NOMINEE,

There is no word for what we are. I have been trying to find the right language to describe us for a long time — are we ex-friends? were you my rival? am I the midlist cuckold, and are you the experimentalist who stole my wife? — but none of it really satisfies. At least that's how I feel about it. We can't be ex-friends, because we never were friends. Not really. We have friends in common, even good ones, but let's be honest: we've never had much of anything to say to each other. Starting at the book party where we met, my book party, when your smugness seemed so weird and inappropriate. It was at a gallery in Chelsea. The room was full of writers, agents, editors, a few artists. I had never heard of you. We were introduced, by the agent who had brought you that night, in the middle of the crowd. *Well,* you seemed to say as we shook hands. *What are* you *doing here?* I shrugged it off as just another bad encounter in the literary world, and I didn't think about it again, or even remember our first meeting, until a few years later, when I realized that you were fucking my wife.

So "rivals" might be getting warmer. It's certainly in the ballpark. Not that I ever considered you my adversary until it was much too late. Looking back now, with the benefit of being broke, I can recall a few more times when I sensed the simian need in you to grab at my banana and scurry with your stolen fruit into the treetops. Do you remember when you introduced me at that reading and sneered that I was a "suburban novelist"? That was the second time you pissed on my pant leg for no reason. But I have never been much for jungle politics. I can see now what a mistake that has been — thinking that I was above the fight for territory, or that I somehow didn't need to protect what was mine.

Yes, I was a cuckold. And yes, you took my wife when you didn't win a prize. Still, that doesn't capture it. You are my son's stepfather, or at least something like it. His anti-narrative dad. Because of the custody agreement I never should have signed that makes me a bystander in my son's life, and only did sign — under duress — so I could be free from all the drama you and Marina created with your insanity, you see my son more than I do. How's that for justice? You listen to his stories about his days at preschool; you watch him polish off another bowl of pasta night after night; you read to him from the crappy Hot Wheels books he picks out from the catalog they slip into his backpack. That's why his bedroom here is empty. Again. That's why I'm sitting here on his candy-striped sheets, next to the penguin humidifier, writing to you.

You've had your say in my life. You are here now. You bullied your way in without an invitation, at least not from me, and you've never, not once, apologized.

Now I get my say. My trip to the winner's podium. That's right: I am taking my prize.

• • •

This letter has been a long time coming. I hadn't planned on writing to you directly, or writing about you at all, to be honest, beyond dropping the nickname you've so richly earned. But I went online the other night to remind myself of what it felt like back when I was in Maryland with the geese and you were climbing the stairs to my apartment with my wife. You know: the apartment you moved into on the same day I moved out. Remember? I saw you carrying in your boxes of books and tubs of Grecian Formula from my U-Haul truck parked across the street. (Okay, so maybe there was no Grecian Formula. I gather that you have never dyed your hair. My bad! You can understand, though, why I thought that shoe-polish sheen came from a jar. We are at the age when age catches up to you.) You knew that I was there. You knew that I was across the street. Funny how you couldn't turn to face me as you shifted on my doorstep. And when Marina put down your box and came running, trying to undo what I'd just witnessed, trying to wash away the reality of it with her tears, you slipped quietly inside the front door and didn't reappear. Soon after that you posed for a publicity photo in my old bedroom. You know the one. You're standing by the window barefoot. In a T-shirt and jeans. Books everywhere. It's a nice picture. The light is flattering. I used to wonder what you were thinking then, what it felt like to just step into someone else's life. To wake up in someone else's bed, with someone else's wife beside you, lying in a furrow in the mattress that you don't quite fill. I didn't check the date of the publicity shot, and I don't feel like doing it now, but I do know that Marina and I were still married when you posed for that picture. It was strange. I had a wife who was living with someone else while she was pregnant with a baby who belonged to me — try *that* sometime — and a marriage binding me to the whole unruly mess that I would have to sue my way out of if I wanted to be free. I didn't think it was possible. I didn't know that any of it was possible. I didn't know that it could happen *period*, let alone that it would happen to me.

So what did you do? How did you make amends? Did you tread softly through the rooms of the apartment? Did you duck from the windows and sit gently in my furniture?

No. You posed for pictures. That's what makes you the Nominee. I'd forgotten about that portrait in your bare feet, sunlight streaming in through the same windows that I used to look out from to check my car on alternate-side parking days, but I'm glad I found it again. It helps me remember what those days felt like, and why it's taken me so long to get my bearings again — to stop looking over my shoulder for what might be lurking behind, to stop checking the bolt on the front door for any signs that someone has been trying to get inside. For signs of attempted larceny.

There are other pictures too. One in particular — you know the one, I'm sure you do — can still bring on a rage years later. The photo on the publishing gossip website from the holiday party that I skipped. Marina and you had just walked in. You had decided, for some reason, to bring my son to the holiday party with you. You had him tucked underneath your arm. He was five weeks old, maybe six. He was dressed in a brown velour onesie. I repeat: you were carrying him. Is it any wonder that the blog identified him as your baby? Think about that: your baby. I suppose I should admire you both for the sheer nerve that it took to bring him to a publishing party and show him off . . . Marina is smiling goofily for the camera. You look smug and shiny with your recent nomination. Primo is bawling, as only an infant can do. His face is twisted with a howl of baby righteousness. He never cried much, not even at that age. But having his picture taken with you and Marina at the holiday party *made him cry*. I loved him for that. It was the only thing that made the picture bearable. He was calling out to me from under your armpit.

Daddy, he was wailing. *I want my daddy, not this guy.*

Let's go back to the night you first groped my wife on the dance floor in your rental tux. At least I'm assuming that's how it started — I'm in the dark when it comes to your courtship with Marina. At this point it no longer matters. I was supposed to call her before I went to bed and find out how the awards had gone. (I was pulling for you that night, if you can believe it. We had the same agent at the time, Leo. How's that for symmetry? Your novel was "difficult," which made it a dark horse. I always like the dark horse. I couldn't get to the bottom of the first page the one and only time I ever tried to read your novel, but I wasn't about to hold that against you. I mean, we were on the same team.) I called Marina that night at 10:00, and again at 11:00, and I called her at 12:00, and I called her at 1:00 A.M. . . . Nothing. I wasn't really worried, though. I mean, I was worried about our marriage, with good reason, and I had started to sense that we were heading for something bad. But I wasn't worried — yet — about someone else. And I had no reason, I thought, to worry about you. You were married, after all. And it looked happy from the outside. I remember a subway ride we all took together one night after being out at the same party in the city. It was late. The F train was crowded. Midnight rush hour. Marina and I leaned into each other by the doors, while you and your wife shared a pole nearby. The train was lurching from stop to stop. At one point, you launched into one of your riffs — about what, I don't remember. You were expansive after a night of drinking, and the mood was right, and you were on a roll. Other people on the subway car started listening in.

I thought, *Now I get why people like him.* But your wife. The incredible way she gazed at you: I can still see it. It was late at night, and she was probably a little drunk too, and she was holding on to the pole in a crowded train that was hardly moving, full of people who just wanted to be home, and it was unmistakable in the way she watched you: the love. I don't need to tell you that your wife was in love with you. It was obvious even on the F train as it crawled and shuddered under the city . . .

I know what it's like to betray someone you love. I know what it's like to be tempted, and to feel that switch inside you that says "yes" go off. It is a terrible thing. The way it eats at you afterward—I guess that's an experience we have in common. It's an area of kinship. I have felt for you, believe it or not. Not often, but I have. I know that my son is crazy about you. His love is something else that we have in common too.

"I just don't think I want to be married anymore."

That's what Marina told me when I finally came home for winter break. It doesn't take wide reading in the literature of extramarital affairs to realize that if your wife sits you down on your front stoop to tell you that she doesn't think she wants to be married anymore, and if this confession has been preceded by lots of trips outside to smoke cigarettes (Marina was only a party smoker), then there is a good chance that she's found someone else to replace you with. That much even I could see.

"Can you tell me who it is?" I asked on the stoop. "I want to know. It's better if I know."

"I can't tell you," she said. "Not yet. It's too hard." She'd been crying, of course, and smoking more American Spirits. The stoop had become scattered with her cigarette butts. It was cold. We were both bundled in our heavy coats. She kept staring off in the distance, down the length of Smith Street. I didn't realize it at the time, but she must have been looking for you. It is possible that you were out there, stooping under a lamppost, or that she was just looking off in the direction of your apartment for comfort. It didn't matter: soon I would be loading up my U-Haul truck, and you would be moving in to pose for pictures. You didn't have to wait long. Just a few more months. Long enough for my first wedding anniversary to pass uncelebrated.

"You need to stop," I told Marina. "Right now."

She looked off across the schoolyard. Smith Street had never looked so desolate. I had found a corner of the neighborhood that they couldn't gentrify. "Okay."

"I can forgive you for this," I remember saying to her. "We can save our marriage. We can work on this and come out of it stronger."

Sniffle. "I know that."

"But you need to stop first. Just *stop*."

"I'll try."

There's only one more thing I'd like to bring up in this letter. All right, maybe two. The first is New Year's Eve. Do you remember the party we all went to? It was in Park Slope. On Tenth Street, I think, in the second-floor apartment of a brownstone. I was not doing well. I had taken Marina's news about our marriage calmly, and I kept on trying to talk her out of leaving me between her yoga engagements, but I felt awful in a way I'd never felt awful before: dizzy, lost, and reeling with pain I couldn't locate. (The dog. I felt like the dog who'd climbed out of that early-morning car crash years before and gone howling up the street.) That was my New Year's Eve. It wasn't a particularly festive party. I'm not saying that because of how I felt, or because a roomful of my friends was suddenly a den of possible adulterers, or because Marina spent most of the night talking with other people, including my friend Noah, who immediately became the prime suspect in my head. It was unfair of me to suspect Noah. He didn't do that sort of thing. I regretted it even while it was happening. But I had nothing else to go on: they were huddled together on the couch, clutching their drinks in red plastic cups, talking quietly and leaning their foreheads close so they could hear each other in the middle of the party. I watched. I tried not to watch. I went over to join them, stupidly. Marina fell quiet as soon as I did, so I backed off and wandered over to a different corner of the party, a different suspect. That was my night. New Year's Eve.

You were there too. A nice bit of choreography. Lurking against the wall in your leather jacket and scanning the party with the gaze of a rigorous formalist in the tradition of B. S. Johnson, William Gaddis, Robert Coover, and Alain Robbe-Grillet. (I got that from Wikipedia: nice entry!) Whose bright idea was it for us to spend New Year's Eve together — the three of us — circling around the truth at the same party? Was it you? Was it Marina's idea? Or did it just sort of, you know, happen? It doesn't really matter now who came up with it. Guess what? I survived. We all have. And we've all paid for it too.

My wife, whom you were fucking, was across the room with Noah. I'm sure I looked just as panicky and as miserable as I felt. I was sitting near the iPod in a folding chair, sipping a bitter glass of champagne, and you came over to say a few words. You know, just to catch up at a party. Two friends. Or rivals. Or strangers. Whatever you want to call us then. Now we're fathers to the same boy.

"But the Mets," you said in your expansive mode, "are a team strangely inclined to fatalism, both in the absolute certainty and the imminence of the end . . ."

I have to admit that I am still baffled by this. I mean, coming over to start a conversation with the husband of the woman you are fucking behind his back? That's too much. You should have just found a way to stay away from me that night. You should have kept to yourself, or found a different New Year's Eve party.

There is one memory I cherish, though. It happened during Primo's first year. His first real spring. I had come out to Carroll Gardens to spend some time with him in the afternoon, as I often did. I met Marina's nanny in the park and took over for her — "He smell you," she used to say. "He know Daddy when he smell 'im." And he did. I used to take him from Georgina's arms, or lift him out of the stroller he was in, and hoist him up in the air under his armpits.

"Primo," I said. That's when I started calling him Primo. He was my first, he was my only, and when I was with him, I didn't care about the drama that you and Marina had created around his birth. It was true then, when he used to grasp my fingers in his hands, wet with drool, and let me help him in the pantomime of walking we used to do up and down the ramp at Carroll Park, and it's still true now that he is four and he runs everywhere in sneakers with blinking heels like satellites. I am his father. He can still smell it on me. Is there any formalism in the world so rigorous as the instinct-life of a baby?

When my allotted time was up that afternoon, I gave him back to Marina, on our usual bench underneath a crooked plane tree. It is a strange feeling, being a part-time parent. One second you are full — there is a life that needs your tending, from help pooing to an untied shoelace to the sudden need for a ham sandwich — and the next, you are empty. But I didn't feel empty that afternoon in Carroll Gardens. As I left the park and walked away down Smith Street, taking the long route down to the F at Bergen Street, I felt full. Bursting, actually. I am almost certain that I was glowing. I was going broke, and that was worrisome. I had lost my way. Had I ever lost my way. But part of me was found. Part of me was happy, maybe even happier than I'd ever been. I had a son who needed me, and I was there for him.

I saw you coming up the street. In my direction. I had been avoiding any situation where our paths might cross — it was too much. It was just too much. I didn't want it. I didn't need the aggravation. When I saw you skulking toward me on the street, I didn't recognize you at first: you were in the late stages of one of your experiments in facial hair — it was a Lemmy, I think. Mutton chops. Just like the guy from Motörhead. You kept coming closer. I stared. I realized that it was you. There was a time when I had relished this opportunity, when I had played it and replayed it in my head: I would see you first, then our eyes would meet, and I would lower my shoulder and slam into your sternum before you had the chance to flinch. That's not how it played out, though. Not at all. Not even close. Remember it? When you saw me coming — and I know you saw me — you turned and hid your face. You hid and pretended you were window-shopping. You hid. It's up for debate whether I should have stopped and given you the lowered shoulder you deserved. I probably should have hit you anyway. Was I afraid? A little. I haven't taken a swing at anyone in earnest since I won a fight, improbably, in the fifth grade. But I saw that I had power over you. I mean, you hid in broad daylight. I was happy that afternoon. I was feeling full. It was my sidewalk. It was my decision. I let you hide and kept on going. I let you hide behind your Lemmy, and it felt good.

Yours sincerely,
The Author

Unpaid Bills

ELIZA HAS BEEN doing her math again. I could feel the numbers riding with us in the taxi on our way home from having dinner with her friends Ana and Marco, tell that she was deep in private computations while I swiped my credit card to pay for the ride and held the door open for her outside our building. I forget that she is not as settled in our life together and as comfortable with its uncertainties as I am. For me, being able to lift an arm on Mercer Street to hail a cab and slide into the seat beside her for a ride that will bounce us over cobblestones and along the shuttered boulevard of Canal Street at night is enough to live on. Looking out the windows at the river of headlights draining down from the Bowery and the Manhattan Bridge while we jostle through traffic and climb past the all-night perfume dealers, the bag merchants, the neon signs in Chinese on the curtained upper floors, and the bright white awning at the summit with its menu of re-enacted spa treatments, and turning to look at Eliza as she quiets the cab's touch screen with a finger and we pick up speed and rattle over the black carpet of the East River — well, it makes me feel like a king. Especially, like tonight, when I know that it's late and the trains will take forever and I have enough room on one of my credit cards—there's $60 on my iTunes Rewards Visa—to pay. When Eliza is busy with her math, the same ride doesn't make her feel much like royalty. I can tell that she is still haunted by the times that I've been broke and couldn't cover the cab fare, by the rent money I've asked her to front for me, by the groceries she's had to buy when the pantry goes bare and the fridge runs empty.

"Can we talk?"

It's later. Eliza has changed into her nightgown after coming home, a short one with a sash and little hearts on it. It is not my favorite of her nightgowns, but I can hardly complain. I've been busy in the kitchen, loading up the dishwasher and wiping the counters with Windex. It's how I keep calm. At least one of the ways. I have an easier time putting my worries to bed and falling asleep, I've found, when I know that the kitchen is spotless.

"Sure," I say. I fold the dishtowel that I've been using to wipe up. "Here or in the living room?"

"Here," she tells me.

"Fine." I lean up against the counter. "Whenever you're ready."

Eliza doesn't say anything for a long time. That's how I know it must be bad. I watch her in the doorway to the kitchen. She's staring at the floor. She has a hard time looking at me. I don't know if this is the end: if this is when she tells me that she's reached her limit, that she can't wait any longer for me to fix my life and find my way. That she's almost thirty-nine and tired of waiting. That she can't listen to another promise; that what she wants is someone who is ready for her, someone who lives in the present tense. Someone who *earns*.

"I need something from you," she says.

"All right."

She lifts her head. "Tell me this is almost over."

I don't say anything.

She pulls the sash on her bathrobe tighter. "Tell me that we can have a home. I want a home I can decorate. I can't look at our cheap window blinds anymore. I've been sleeping on a bed without a headboard since we moved in together, Ben. It has *wheels*. I need you to tell me that we can buy a nicer bed. Really soon. I know I can't go on living this way."

"I can't do that," I say.

She freezes. I watch her deflate.

"I'm broke," I tell her.

"That part I know," she says.

"Stay right there."

I go into the front hallway and find my shoulder bag. There's a pocket inside where I keep all the unpaid bills I pull from the mailbox before Eliza can see them: the collection notices disguised as paychecks, the credit card statements I will never open, the slender threats with cellophane windows and Texas in the return address. I take what's there and bring the bills back into the kitchen. I put them down on the counter for Eliza to see.

"Wait," I say. "There's more."

From there I go into the bedroom. I pull the top drawer of my dresser open and I reach under the balled-up socks, push aside the pairs of briefs I never wear. I have another stash of bills I've been keeping here to age: parking tickets, bills from doctors and hospitals, an old landline that I used to use for phone interviews. Most of the envelopes are still sealed. I bring them into the kitchen and I add them to the pile on the counter. It is my past. I am showing it to her. I am not hiding anything.

"There," I say. "That's everything. It's worse than I admitted."

The counter is gleaming. We stand there looking at the pile

I've unearthed. I have never seen so many unpaid bills—so many outstanding debts—in one place. It is a relief, somehow. A benediction of all that I have borrowed, all that I owe.

"I can't promise you a bed," I tell Eliza.

"No," she says. "I can see that."

"I can't buy new blinds either," I say.

Her voice gets quiet. "You should have told me."

"I probably can't afford to keep you."

She looks up. The little hearts on her nightgown are swimming. I have not been able to buy her the engagement ring: I haven't even had it in me to go back to the boutique for a visit. The $9,100 it costs might as well be $91,000 or $91 million—the number has the same ice-cold gleam of the unattainable. Like a lover who is about to leave.

"Why didn't you tell me?"

I understand now. I have no idea why it took me so long. It's not about the money. It isn't about the window blinds either, or the bed with wheels. Eliza isn't leaving me—if she is about to leave—because of anything that I can't afford to buy for her, not even an engagement ring. Money can be made. Debts can be settled. I will find a way to write again.

But what about the symmetry?

Old Friends

HOW MUCH OF OUR lives do we write, and how much of them are written for us? I've been thinking about this problem lately, looking back over the trail that brought me to this place, and reading my progress at every step along the way — as adrift as I have been from the usual compass points, as unaware of my direction — for signs of an author, for the fingerprints left behind by some great invisible hand. My life is not a story. It has never been a story, not for me, not even while I've been taking great pains with this testament to tell it truthfully on the page. I am in too deep to call it a story. It *hurts* too much for me to understand it. But I am trying. I have been trying all along. I can say this: there is something in me that has wasted too much time in longing, an instinct that has whispered in my ear, tugged me by the sleeve, kept me circling back into the pages of a story that I didn't write myself. I've got a copy of it right here, actually. It's on paper. My father sent the story to me not too long ago, in manuscript. The events it describes all happened forty years ago, and the people who matter most in it — my parents — have put forty years in trying to rectify the mistakes and the losses the story dissects, forty years of distance between themselves and the young married couple they used to be.

This is what my father writes in his cover letter:

Dear Ben,

I found this story filed away with my divorce decree, "Certificate of Divorce Absolute," a few days ago. I had forgotten about writing it. It is the last piece of fiction I wrote before a 19-year hiatus. I must have completed it shortly after your mother and I divorced, early in 1972.

I thought you might find it of interest.

The story has a title that doesn't quite fit: "Old Friends." At least that's what I would say if I were just a reader and not a character in the story too. I can tell that my father wrote it on the green Hermes portable that sat in front of the window in his living room in Gloucester the whole time I was growing up, the same typewriter that he used for writing the letters and notes to us that arrived regularly in the mail. In broad strokes, "Old Friends" is the anatomy of a divorce between a writer and his young wife, with the Vietnam War and the political upheaval of the late 1960s and early 1970s as backdrop. It's told in the third person (the writer is referred to as "the husband" or "the writer," while his wife is called "the wife"), though there is little else I can find that makes the story fiction. Other than the "old friend," who is an invention partly based on an old friend of my mother's at the time, an exaggerated device for bringing out conflict. The writer is my father, the wife is my mother, the oldest son is my brother, and the twins are my sister and me. The old friend in the title is the wife's childhood friend, a painter who is trying to break away from her blue-blood family and raise her consciousness at a commune in Mendocino. She is free; the couple is not.

They feel trapped in the circumstances that life has given them. The writer is struggling with his work, a long novel that he can't seem to write, anxious about their lack of money, lost in despair about the war in Vietnam. The wife regrets having left college to start a family so young and she is working to support the husband while he tries to live the life of a writer. She regrets that too, and wonders about the freedom she has given up at such an early age — the roles she is stuck in as "wife" and "mother." The old friend's visits to see the couple are the trope that marks the changes in their lives, exposing the fault lines in their marriage, one by one, their desperation as the family comes apart.

In the story's first visit, the old friend plops herself down in the fraying red butterfly chair. I remember that chair. I can still smell the canvas of its cover, the same smell as a rainy day. She stretches her long legs out on the worn braided rug, under windows without curtains, and shares how happy she is to be finished with college and out in the world with so much to experience.

"Bitch," the wife remarks to the writer once the old friend has left. She is pregnant again after a three-year respite. In the fall, the story tells us, the couple will learn that she is carrying twins. They have given up their health insurance to save money and they don't know how they're going to pay the doctors' bills. The husband's guilt about their financial problems turns him inward, and his troubles are a bellwether:

> Often he despaired, often he could not work, shouted horribly at his wife who had to have the patience for three; often he just sat around and moped or got up and walked endlessly at the sea's edge by himself, coming home smelling of it and going into his study, which was also their bedroom, where she would come upon him sitting in front of a pile of manila manuscript paper, some of which he would hold up in front of him seeming

to stare through it, as though there were an invisible hole in it, a window on their bedroom window on the driveway, on the water beyond the trees.

A year passes. The twins are born. The couple moves to a bigger house and they are up to their elbows in diapers. The tension between them has grown worse, their arguments more frequent and intractable. The husband grows so angry during one fight about making lunch that he picks up a deck chair and throws it at his wife; when she comes home from the hospital with stitches underneath her braided hair, he collapses on his knees and begs forgiveness. The wife's skin has stretched from carrying twins and she complains of feeling used up and unattractive; they discuss seeing a plastic surgeon to have it fixed but they can't afford the $2,000 it would cost to have the procedure done, or justify something so frivolous at a time when, around the world in Vietnam, women and children are being killed and maimed by the U.S. government, burned alive with napalm. With so much stress and constant fighting in the house, the babies are not sleeping.

The old friend arrives for her annual visit to the East Coast and sprawls herself out on their lawn in a bikini. She regales the couple with her newly formed opinions on Eldridge Cleaver, the Peace and Freedom Party, Richard Brautigan, and the new American imperialism. She pays little mind to the children. She remarks to the wife that she looks worn out and tells them about her new life in Oakland. When she finally leaves, the wife is inconsolable. She accuses the husband of having ogled their old friend in her bikini while they discussed Norman Mailer's *The Armies of the Night* and she was busy breast-feeding hungry twins.

She's not my type, he said, trying to deflect her anger.

Anything's better than me right now.

Let's go see the plastic surgeon about your stomach, he said.

See, she shouted, *you do really mind it. You're disturbed by it —*

I am because you are.

I don't believe you, she cried.

You have to —

No, I don't —

But I love you —

You're just stuck with me now and you have to make yourself believe you do.

Another year passes. This time the old friend writes from Mendocino with a parcel of news. She's met someone at the commune, a man who just walked into her life one day, and they're buying some property on the beach to build a house on. Her days are filled with plans for the house, the painting studio she wants to construct, their garden. "Again I'm sitting in the warm winter sun by the funky ocean, the sea, everything crisp and clear," she writes in a flourish. When the letter arrives, the husband is home with the children. He reads the letter and puts it aside. He brings it to his wife on his next visit to see her in the psychiatric unit of a hospital nearby. One night not too long before, after bathing the three children and putting them to bed, the husband came downstairs and found his wife in a ball on the kitchen floor, sobbing and heaving silently. After reviving with a cup of tea, she confesses that she has been hoarding sleeping pills and tranquilizers for months on end and that she has been planning on driving into the woods nearby, taking as many of the pills as she can, and lying down to die. The wife hasn't been eating. She has lost so much weight that her clothes hang loosely from her body; she is exhausted when she returns from her job and no longer has energy for taking care of the children — or herself. The husband has checked her into the hospital and taken over parenting duties full-time. He feeds them their meals, gets them dressed, takes the oldest off to kindergarten, keeps the twins busy, feeds them all supper, bathes them at night, gets them ready for bed, then wakes up and starts all over again.

The unit seems to be helping, though. If not with their marriage, then at least with her depression. On the day the husband brings the letter from the old friend to the hospital, his wife is dressed like herself again in a pair of bell-bottom dungarees and a purple leotard. She wears a gold kerchief in her hair for the special occasion, teak hoop earrings that she hasn't put on since the husband first courted her. The children have come along for the visit too. She gives each of them a small present that she's bought for them on an outing to Cambridge, and she shows off a pair of new walking shoes that she found at a boutique. On the way back home in the car, the children bubble about the visit while the husband listens in.

But Mommy's not really sick, he heard his daughter insist to her brothers in the backseat. *She said she doesn't hurt on her body. That's why she isn't in bed!* the second son replied triumphantly. *They're gonna let her come home pretty soon. She said so.*

She's just sad, said his oldest son with a crack in his voice that told him he had intuited everything.

I knew Mum was sad, his daughter said. *She used to go in her room a lot and cry. Why was she sad, Dad? Was it because you both yelled at each other all the time? Why did you yell at each other? Don't you love each other anymore?*

The husband starts to give her an answer, but the children are already absorbed in their comic books and he loses himself in sadness while he drives home.

There's one more scene from my father's short story that needs recounting. A few more weeks have passed. The wife is still in the hospital, though her release looks certain at this point. She's decided to divorce the husband. He is resigned to it and even agrees that divorce is probably for the best. She will take care of the children, and he will go back to living a solitary life. One night on a walk, the husband recalls a day that summer when the children had come screeching inside from the yard to tell him that something was wrong in the garden. The wife had spent the spring reading books about organic gardening, having their soil tested, planning what vegetables to plant, and preparing all the garden beds herself. It was her project, and she hadn't wanted anyone's help. She had ended up planting a spectacular garden: carrots and tomato vines, beans on slender poles, rows of tall corn, purple cabbages, lettuce, and pumpkins. That afternoon, when she had gone out to weed and pick some lettuce for their supper, she had discovered that someone — kids from the neighborhood, most likely — had stomped on the corn and lettuce, pulled up the carrots, torn the green tomatoes from their vines, and knocked the bean poles to the ground. The children were frantic. The husband had followed them out to inspect the damage and talk to his wife about what had happened. But he couldn't find her anywhere. He had been about to go inside and call the police when he saw his wife standing alone under an oak tree nearby, sobbing hard but quietly, without making a noise — the same silent sobbing that had frightened him so much when he found her on the kitchen floor. He had gone to her then. So had the children. They rushed to her and took hold of whatever part of her they could grab — the children all clung together to her legs — and they held on to her with all of their strength, trying to keep her there, trying to love her, trying to convince her with the force of their grasp that she was safe and everything was not lost. The story goes on:

> In fact they had been able to repair the damage, to save most of the vegetables. Each night shortly thereafter they sent the children down for lettuce. The cabbages came, and even later the bright orange pumpkins, some of which were still piled in the cellar. Ultimately they had all rejoiced in and shared the garden. But as he stood now over the garden's ruins, he realized just how hopeless his wife's cries had been, for they must have come from a sense of things broken and gone awry far deeper and more subtle, far crueler and more painful than boys spoiling her handiwork, trampling on the things she'd given life to . . .

I remember that oak tree where we mobbed my mother that day. Where we held on to her so tightly — all of us — because we wanted her to feel better about the garden, we wanted her to live. But we also held on to her for selfish reasons, to feel safe from the dangers that were closing in around our family. If we could just hold her under the oak tree for long enough, pin her there with our arms and legs, then maybe disaster would never reach us. I used to go back to that oak tree when I got older without knowing why. I had never read my father's story. I didn't remember the garden and my mother's tears. It was an old pain. It was ancient already. My mother had gone back to school as soon as we moved to Cambridge and managed somehow to raise three kids at the same time that she was working up the ladder from a bachelor's degree in night school to a PhD. The father I knew preached nonviolence to the point of boredom and literally wouldn't hurt a wasp; I used to watch him trap them at the window in summer-time and carry them gingerly outside with a pair of pasta tongs. My brother and sister and I have a running joke that our father has become "the happiest man alive." Still, something kept drawing me back to that ruined garden that I no longer remembered. My mother's garden from forty years ago. I would go there and stand in the shelter of the oak tree and let the strangest feelings wash over me. It was like fear, but there was nothing to be afraid of there. I felt sad, but I didn't have a reason. I kept going back to that barren spot underneath the oak tree and I never knew why — why I stood there stupidly, with my hands in my pockets — other than to find that feeling again.

It took my own life turning into a story that I didn't choose, my own episode in the garden, before I could find my way back to the place where I first knew love and all its trampled feelings, the mortal danger that comes with being here, the one patch of earth where I started life, and keep returning. That's what symmetry is: an appetite to return. I am trying to get over it. I am trying to stop losing. I am trying to stop pleading to every love I have:

Please.

Don't leave.

The Tower Where I Work

IT'S BEEN A WHILE since I came into your room and wrote to you. A couple of months, I guess, though it feels this morning like it's been longer. It's springtime. I don't have to tell you this. We have been talking about it when I walk you down the hill to preschool, on Eighth Street, from the subway in the morning: how the crocuses come up first, pushing their swords through the snow, followed by the daffodils and the other early-rising flowers in the yards behind the gates, the buried planters and neglected gardens in front of every brownstone. The snow has melted. So have the last black islands of soot and ice on the sidewalks, the shrunken snowdrifts that are the city's greatest insult to the winter. Even you don't want to climb them. "Do you know what that is?" I asked you one morning on the way to school. You were riding on my shoulders with your backpack on. It was muggy out. We were waiting for the light to change on Seventh Avenue and I looked down to see a ridge of ice so infused with city grime that it had become another substance. There were chicken bones inside, a paper plate from Smiling Pizza. "What is it, Daddy?" you asked. "What?" "That's a New York–flavored popsicle," I said. You liked that joke. You squealed about it down the block to school. "A *popsicle*?" I held your ankles tighter to keep you from keeling over. "There's no popsicle that tastes like New York, Daddy!"

Maybe I am imagining things, but when we got to your classroom and I stowed your backpack away in your cubby, next to a clique of girls trying on outfits from the costume chest and your best friend, Henry, a boy of furious emotions from the Kazakh Steppe, munching on a bagel slice at the snack table — you hung back. You didn't want to let me go. When we say our good-byes at your cubby in the morning, it is not just until the end of the day; you will go home to a different house to have your dinner and your bath and your stories at bedtime, and you will close your eyes with another family swimming in your head. Your bed in my house will be made and ready for your next visit, just as it is now, and I have no idea if you will replay our last wave through the classroom window, the kiss you blow me from inside before I leave the Big Yard and head back to the subway. You have your own way of doing it, a variation you made up yourself: first you plant a kiss on your palm, then you throw it off and let it go like a butterfly, and finally, you blow. I don't know if you ever think of our good-byes in your other house, or if you've ever wondered, as you retrace the path of your kiss from the cup of your hand into the air that carries it past the empty aquarium where the flock of chicks from the farm hatched, and over the activity table to the window where I'm standing on the other side and looking in, how a kiss can travel that far. They can. Yours do. When you get older and you look back on this time for clues about how you were made and molded — it happens to all of us, eventually — how much of what I've written down here will you remember? If the hours that we've spent together up to now could be measured in a quantity, how much have you forgotten? What proportion is already gone? What tiny sliver of the whole have I saved by getting out of bed while it's still dark and Eliza is still sleeping and coming into your room to write these lines for you?

I don't have long this morning. I will try to make this entry brief and to the point. You see, the sun is coming up. It's still quiet outside your bedroom windows. The sky is filling up with a morning shade of blue, and the big white warehouse with the water tower, the brick apartment buildings in the distance, and the shiny new condo towers faced in glass have all begun to glow and rise from Brooklyn's tree cover like the Mayan ruins at Tulum. I have missed this time of day. The ritual of rising early, making coffee at the stove, and carrying it down the hallway while the cat stalks me and croaks for his first breakfast. Opening my notebook on your bed to the last full page and reading over what I've written the day before. Lifting the pen to the next empty line and starting with a phrase. Or even less: a word. Writing it in the hope that it will one day reach you, wherever you may be in life, and that the words that I've been pulling from the sunrise and the city's quiet breathing while it sleeps will be a help to you when you need it, will make your origins (it's a big word, I know) a little less mysterious. Mine have had too much power over me, in large part, I have come to believe, because they were a secret. Now they are not. I didn't know that I have been missing something for all these years, a story — there is no better word — that I lived through but could not remember because it happened so long ago. A story about what it was like at the beginning, when our garden was stomped, and there was something in my mother that couldn't be consoled, and the world was heaving beneath our feet. I can see now that I have been returning to that ruined garden on my own, far too often and for much too long. I have gone back to that garden in search of comfort that I couldn't find anywhere else, and it has cost me.

So I've been away, it's true. I have left these pages alone to season. To steep quietly in their hiding place. Normally this retreat to silence would be a bad sign. Another plunge into dreaming, another project left midstream, more debt at an even higher interest rate. More life burned away by staring into screens, those carriers of ancient shadows that we take with us now, everywhere — they are the cave, the fire, and the dancing figures on the wall, all shrunk to fit inside a pocket, to nestle in the hand, sleek and portable and gleaming. This time it's different, though. The silence, I mean. You see, I have started to wake up. I am snapping out of the spell. Or is it a slumber? A daze? I don't know what to call it. My unraveling. I'm sure there is a syndrome with a name and an acronym to describe the phenomenon of getting lost in too much life, a drug cocktail for leading you out of the woods and guiding you back to that deep and rugged road again. I've found another way back: I am working. That's right, I am on payroll. It's temporary for the time being, a four-month contract at a magazine that's short-staffed after the cutbacks and buyouts of the Great Media Retraction, but there is a chance, at the end, that they will keep me on. In the meantime, I can pay my bills. I am still in debt. My phone still vibrates with calls from dyslexic-looking area codes, though they tend to reach out during regular business hours now instead of in the dead of night, or first thing in the morning. The flow of collection "telegrams" and envelopes emblazoned with the warnings "personal" and "urgent" has slowed to a trickle. Every dollar that I take in is spoken for when it lands in my account on Thursdays, and I hardly get to enjoy the influx on my computer screen, ogle my wealth via online banking, before it vanishes into the upsurge of capital. I still dip into overdraft. I still *owe*. More than I take in. But it is not getting any worse, and I am grateful for that. I have managed to stop the bleeding.

I am a fact-checker. That's my job. That's what I get paid for every week. It is a humble position in the magazine world, with no glamour or prestige attached, a kind of editorial support — it is important work but too little valued. Fact-checkers make sure that every statement in an article can be proven and backed up, that the captions describe the right photos, that the photos are of the right person, or place, or recipe. In the past I would have called it a step backward. An embarrassing one, even. Writers are fact-checked, most often, in my experience, by an aspiring writer from Williamsburg or the Lower East Side with an expensive liberal arts degree that hasn't done them any measurable good and too many roommates for the loft space or railroad they live in. Once you've earned your own byline, there is someone else in a cluttered cubicle who gets paid to verify your dates and geography, square all your citations, call anyone you've quoted to check their names and make sure you haven't taken any liberties. Right now, that someone in the cubicle is me. I have a headset that fits snugly on my ear and my own phone extension. I have an e-mail address and an employee number. I am in Research, so the more exalted editors, higher on the masthead, generally look right through me. There are stations in life, and this is mine until my contract ends. I am happy with it. I enjoy the work. I am aware that, according to the given rules, mine is not the sort of job you're meant to have and to appreciate if you've published books and you're forty-two. But I see it differently, I guess. When you have counted out your change before your son's eyes because you need to buy him dinner, or felt the thud of the locked subway turnstile against your legs when your MetroCard runs empty, status and station — well, they don't mean a whole lot. At least they don't to me. I am not worried anymore about appearances. There is even a kind of poetic justice, I think, in winding up at a fact-checker's desk, when for much too long I have wasted time and energy — not that I've been fully aware of it — with trying to

be TOO GOOD TO BE TRUE. The facts have been my problem. I
have let them get the better of me. Now I am getting paid to check
them, and I count that as a good thing.

I start my days by going underground to the decrepit stations and screeching subway cars that keep our city humble, the
pockets of unnatural temperature on the train platforms and the
ancient pillars that look somehow dirtier with each new coat of
municipal paint. There among the sip cups and the high-tech
tote bags, the copies of the same five paperbacks that everyone
is reading, the BlackBerrys and the iPads and the Kindles with
their sleeves that open up like book covers — sneaky — I wait. I
am happiest when I wait with you. When there are two legs to my
commute. When we rush through the turnstile and down into
the station because I let you sleep and you were slow with your
breakfast and you kept on diving on your bed when it was time to
get dressed and now we're running late for school. "Slow *down*,
Daddy," you say. I'm tugging you through the station to the platform, trying to hurry so we won't miss the next train. Your small
moist hand is in mine. I am distracted, lost in routes and calcula-
tions. "My legs are tired," you complain. "Daddy! You aren't listening to me!" On the platform, I kneel down and slip your backpack off. You are sweating. I lift you in my arms then, and we peer
down the tracks for the first sign of headlights deep inside the
tunnel, the shining on the rails when the G train rounds its turn
and heads into the station before us. "Is it coming, Daddy?" you
ask, leaning out farther over the tracks. "Do you see it?" "Keep
watching," I say. "We'll see it." No one ever told me, before I became a father — that is, before I had you — just how physical the
love between a parent and a child is. How it is a passion of its
own. It starts all the way back, I suppose, when you arrived as
an infant. I fed you bottles of breast milk with a layer of cream at
the top, I bathed you in warm water that must have felt like the

womb, I wiped you clean of your own filth and changed diapers that smelled so bad they made me dizzy, I sang the "Cu-Cù" song to you when you wouldn't sleep, and I leaned over your crib in the middle of the night, if things got too quiet, and listened for your breathing. Babies are flesh. With big beholding eyes. Every one of them is a foundling left on the doorstep with a note that reads, *Please take care of this child.* To survive, they seduce you. I'm bringing all this up now to say one thing. I really meant it when I told you that this entry wouldn't take long. It's getting lighter out, and Eliza's alarm will start tolling in the bedroom soon, and I need to put the kettle on for her first cup of tea before I head into the shower and start getting ready for the office. It's this: on the mornings when I leave for the station without you, my hands feel empty. My arms want something to carry. I didn't know before I had you that I could miss a child's hand in mine, forty pounds of wriggling boy on my shoulders. I didn't know that I could long for it. But I do. Sometimes, I do.

The tower where I work is a marvel in the Midtown sky. It's so brand-new that, when I come up from underground and start walking to it through the obstacle course of slow-moving tourists and phone addicts getting their fix, passing through construction awnings and under flashing billboards and around gaping holes left in the street, it looks too pristine to be real. It hovers over the broken city underneath it like an obelisk — stories of glass climbing skyward, protected by a gleaming metal skin. I have not spent much time in skyscrapers, or appreciated what I can now see is their beauty. They have a kind of longing built into them too, if you're attuned to it. They have aspirations. They have *depths.* The tower where I work? It wants to be permanent. It wants to last a hundred years and maybe more; it wants to stand on Eighth Avenue with its needle touching the clouds while the rest of the city goes on knocking itself down and rebuilding, carting off the rubble and starting again from sunlight and dirt, the empty space New York keeps padlocked behind walls of blue plywood. I arrive at the tower and walk in through the doors. They are tall and glass and much too heavy—maybe they are bombproof—but with a little bit of effort, they swing open. The lobby is always hushed. Its color scheme is warm and soothing. The room emits a low, ambient hum from an art installation hanging in the gallery between the elevator banks, and a grove of birch trees sits nestled in a hillock behind glass, an atrium with wild green grasses and a boardwalk running through. Do you know what they make me think of? The trees and their wooden boardwalk, I mean? When I glimpse the Imprisoned Forest on my way across the lobby to the security turnstiles and the "smart" elevators that will carry me to my fact-checking cubicle? It was last summer, in mid-August, I think, and we were at the house in Maine. Gotts Island. It was dark outside and getting foggy, and it was already past your bedtime. I'd zipped you in your warmest set of PJs and won the nightly battle to get your teeth brushed, and I'd read you stories on the couch with the woodstove ticking and Eliza cozy on your other side—just the way you liked it then. The only thing left in our nightly routine was to go outside and take one last pee together. When you were little and we used to do it in Brooklyn, outside your favorite playground, we called it "watering the trees." You asked to use your new flashlight. Do you remember the one I'm talking about? Maybe you do. It was the one that your grandma and *méme* found for you: it strapped around your forehead and you wore it like a cave explorer's lantern. You loved that flashlight. You wore it everywhere that week. I could hardly get it off you, until the strap broke. I buckled you in outside on the porch. I could smell the fog and hear the ocean. The tide was low. "Is that good?" I asked you. "Good," you said. I turned on the power and I let you lead the way. I followed you.

I had a lot on my mind that night. Things that weighed, felt heavy. If you can remember the night I mean, the one I've been telling you about, that's why I took my time going down the stairs and let you go ahead. I needed a little space. Earlier that day, while you and Eliza were down on the rocks exploring tide pools, I had gone off in search of reception bars so I could check my e-mail. I was waiting to hear about a job—a good one, with university benefits—and I knew I'd made it to the final round. It was down to the last two candidates, and I was feeling hopeful. I had prepared an extensive memo full of ideas for how to improve the program, and the last stages of the interview process had gone well. The bad news came at a clearing in the woods: *I'm sorry that it's taken so long to get back to you. The search committee finally had a chance to meet and chose another candidate with more management experience and a PhD. It was a very difficult decision, and I am grateful for the time and energy you put in during the search . . .* I hadn't told Eliza yet. I was waiting for the right moment. It would be hard news to deliver, and I needed time to prepare. We had just moved in together—just joined our lives—and it would worry her, I knew. It would start her on another cycle of doubt and fear and questioning, and I would find myself making promises to her that I wasn't sure if I could keep—vows that I was about to turn it around and make myself solvent again. If only she could wait for me. The night had started out clear, with a faint wash of stars. Now the fog was rolling in off the water and blanketing everything in mist: it was pouring into the yard over the brush piles on the bank, swamping the blackberry bushes and the tall, wild grass, climbing high into the tree branches. I was afraid. I can remember what it felt like. It was a cold, creeping realization in my belly that nothing had to change, that I might stay broke, that I could go on writing things to death and never finishing what I started. That I would go on having you as a son on a part-time schedule that I didn't choose, and I would lose Eliza because she couldn't wait — she had a better life in mind. I turned back to the house and watched it in the fog. It looked warm and safe from the yard. The kerosene lamps were lit inside, and I knew that Eliza was reading by the fire in her flannel pajamas and SmartWool socks. The stove would be ticking. The flames in the lamps would be staining the glass chimneys black. I went away for a while. I lost myself again. I was in a place so old it doesn't have a name. When I came back to the yard in the thickening fog, back to the house with its glowing windows, listening while a foghorn made a sad, long moan across the water, I turned around again and looked for you. I held my breath. You had not gone far. I saw your flashlight in the fog, shining in a solid beam. You were standing at the place where the yard met the woods, pointing your flashlight up into the trees above your head, running the light over their outstretched arms to inspect them, down along their crooked trunks and into the grass, and deeper into the spruce woods. You were not lost. I was looking out for you. The fog was thick and it kept rolling in, the darkness of the woods was looming all around you. I know that you will wander in someday. It's inevitable in this life. There are shadows there to draw you deeper than you meant to go, voices that will leave you spellbound. I will not be there to stop you. I will not be there to call your name and make you turn back. There will be the woods, and there will be you. A boy with a flashlight.

About the Author

BENJAMIN ANASTAS IS the author of *An Underachiever's Diary* (hailed by Very Short List as "the funniest, most underappreciated book of the 1990s") and *The Faithful Narrative of a Pastor's Disappearance*, a *New York Times* Notable Book. He lives in Brooklyn, New York.